Andrew Manship

National Jewels: Washington, Lincoln, and the fathers of the revolution

Andrew Manship

National Jewels: Washington, Lincoln, and the fathers of the revolution

ISBN/EAN: 9783743311367

Manufactured in Europe, USA, Canada, Australia, Japa

Cover: Foto ©ninafisch / pixelio.de

Manufactured and distributed by brebook publishing software (www.brebook.com)

Andrew Manship

National Jewels: Washington, Lincoln, and the fathers of the revolution

TO

LIEUTENANT-GENERAL GRANT,

This Volume is Dedicated,

AS A TOKEN OF THE PROFOUND RESPECT

OF THE

COMPILER

FOR HIS INVALUABLE SERVICES IN CONDUCTING

THE ARMIES OF THE UNION IN TRIUMPH

THROUGH THE LATE DREADFUL WAR.

PREFACE.

Now that the gigantic Rebellion which persistently held out for four long years, spreading desolation throughout the whole country, East West, North, and South, forcibly reminding us of the passage, "In Rama was there a voice heard, lamentation and weeping, and great mourning, Rachel weeping for her children and would not be comforted, because they are not:" now that the rebellion is happily over, should not all, in every portion of the country, pray for a permanent peace, and that Christ, the King of kings and Lord of lords, may so reign on this green, beautiful earth, that "nation shall not lift up sword against nation, neither shall they learn war any more"? In some cases, however—

> "Perhaps war is but Heaven's great ploughshare, driven
> Over the barren, fallow earthly fields,
> Preparing them for harvest; rooting up
> Grass, weeds, and flowers, which necessary fall,
> That in these furrows the wise husbandman
> May drop celestial seed."

I have asked myself the question, What can I do in order to benefit my redeemed, beloved country, of which I can enthusiastically say—

> "Long may our land be bright
> With freedom's holy light?"

In answering this important question, I have settled down on this point: That I can do good by arranging and presenting in an inviting form the great patriotic sentiments of our national benefactors, "of whom the world was not worthy;" and last, but by no means least, in this bright galaxy we place our martyred illustrious successor of the great immortal Washington, the Father of his country. His Inaugurals show good-will to all sections of his beloved country, and "malice towards none." What he has said, as set forth in this unpretending volume, will be read by generations now unborn, and all will be ready to say, "What could have been done more to my vineyard, that I have not done in it? Wherefore, when I looked that it should bring forth grapes, brought it forth wild grapes?" But "surely the wrath of man shall praise Thee:" and though the Government at the head of which Mr. Lincoln was providentially placed did not expect or desire to interfere with the existing arrangements and institutions of the country, the Rebellion of our southern brethren brought forth the Emancipation Proclamation, and has necessarily and forever abolished slavery. Yes, one effect of the war has been to "undo the heavy burdens and to let the oppressed go free;" to vindicate the principle that liberty is the birthright of every man; and to make that part of the glorious old Declaration of Independence that says "all men are created equal," consistent and harmonious with the facts in the case.

Finally, I feel assured that those into whose hands this volume may fall will not object to the religious portion of the compilation. We gratefully remember that our Fathers in the old State House in Philadelphia, when about signing the Declaration of Independence that brought down upon them the anathemas of crowned heads and thrones, felt the need of God's blessing, and called in a venerable minister of religion to read the Bible and pray to the God of nations for his benediction on the great work in which those patriotic hearts were about to engage. The readers of this volume will not forget "Happy is that nation whose God is the Lord;" and while they will readily agree that there are national jewels contained in this work, they will not deny that our Lord's Sermon on the Mount is a DIVINE JEWEL, a pearl of great price; and should its precepts sink deeply into the hearts of my fellow-countrymen, and of all the people of the earth, then the shout would be heard everywhere, "Glory to God in the highest, and on earth peace, good-will toward men." Praise God that "this cruel war is over" in our own country, and we will now unite in adopting the language of the Prophet and say, "O Lord, revive thy work in the midst of the years, in the midst of the years make known; in wrath remember mercy," and in our approaches to God we will say—

> "Strike with thy bolt the next red flag unfurled,
> And make all wars to cease throughout the world."

A. MANSHIP.

CONTENTS.

I. Declaration of Independence	9
II. Constitution of the United States, including the proposed Constitutional Amendment	15
III. Correspondence of Bishops Asbury and Coke with President Washington	34
IV. Washington's Farewell Address	37
V. Reception of Mr. Lincoln in Independence Hall	56
VI. First Inaugural Address of Abraham Lincoln	58
VII. Announcement of the Proclamation of Emancipation	69
VIII. Proclamation of Emancipation	73
IX. Address of the General Conference to President Lincoln, with the Reply of the President	76
X. Second Inaugural Address of Abraham Lincoln	79
XI. Funeral Solemnities at the White House, Washington	82
XII. Funeral Oration of Bishop Simpson at Springfield	96
XIII. National Hymns:	
"The Star-Spangled Banner"	112
"Our God is Marching On" (battle Hymn of the Republic)	113
XIV. A DIVINE JEWEL! The Lord's Sermon on the Mount	114

THE DECLARATION OF INDEPENDENCE.

WHEN, in the course of human events, it becomes necessary for one people to dissolve the political bands which have connected them with another, and to assume, among the powers of the earth, the separate and equal station to which the laws of nature and of nature's God entitle them, a decent respect to the opinions of mankind requires that they should declare the causes which impel them to the separation.

We hold these truths to be self-evident, that all men are created equal; that they are endowed by their Creator with certain unalienable rights; that among these, are life, liberty, and the pursuit of happiness. That, to secure these rights, governments are instituted among men, deriving their just powers from the consent of the governed; that, whenever any form of government becomes destructive of these ends, it is the right of the people to alter or to abolish it, and to institute a new government, laying its foundation on such principles, and organizing its powers in such form, as to them shall seem most likely to effect their safety and happiness. Prudence, indeed, will dictate that governments long established, should not be changed for light and transient causes; and, accordingly, all experience hath shown, that mankind are more disposed to suffer, while evils are sufferable, than to right themselves by abolishing the forms to which they are accustomed. But, when a long train of abuses and usurpations, pursuing invariably the same object, evinces a design to reduce them under absolute despotism, it is their right, it is their duty, to throw off such government, and to provide new guards for their future security. Such has been the patient sufferance of these colonies, and such is now the necessity which constrains them to alter their former systems of government. The history of the present king of Great Britain is a history of repeated injuries and usurpations, all having, in direct object, the establishment of an absolute tyranny over these States. To prove this, let facts be submitted to a candid world:

He has refused his assent to laws the most wholesome and necessary for the public good.

He has forbidden his Governors to pass laws of immediate and pressing importance, unless suspended in their operation till his assent should be obtained; and, when so suspended, he has utterly neglected to attend to them.

He has refused to pass other laws for the accommodation of large districts of people, unless those people would relinquish the right of representation in the legislature; a right inestimable to them, and formidable to tyrants only.

He has called together legislative bodies at places unusual, uncomfortable, and distant from the depository of their public records, for the sole purpose of fatiguing them into compliance with his measures.

He has dissolved representative houses repeatedly, for opposing, with manly firmness, his invasions on the rights of the people.

He has refused, for a long time after such dissolutions, to cause others to be elected; whereby the legislative powers, incapable of annihilation, have returned to the people at large for their exercise; the State remaining, in the mean time, exposed to all the danger of invasion from without, and convulsions within.

He has endeavored to prevent the population of these States; for that purpose, obstructing the laws for naturalization of foreigners; refusing to pass others to encourage their migration hither, and raising the conditions of new appropriations of lands.

He has obstructed the administration of justice, by refusing his assent to laws for establishing judiciary powers.

He has made judges dependent on his will alone, for the tenure of their offices, and the amount and payment of their salaries.

He has erected a multitude of new offices, and sent hither swarms of officers to harass our people, and eat out their substance.

He has kept among us, in times of peace, standing armies, without the consent of our legislature.

He has affected to render the military independent of, and superior to, the civil power.

He has combined, with others, to subject us to a jurisdiction foreign to our constitution, and unacknowledged by our laws; giving his assent to their acts of pretended legislation:

For quartering large bodies of armed troops among us:

For protecting them, by a mock trial, from punishment, for any murders which they should commit on the inhabitants of these States:

For cutting off our trade with all parts of the world:

For imposing taxes on us without our consent:

For depriving us, in many cases, of the benefits of trial by jury:

For transporting us beyond seas to be tried for pretended offences:

For abolishing the free system of English laws in a neighboring province, establishing therein an arbitrary government, and enlarging its boundaries, so as to render it at once an example and fit instrument for introducing the same absolute rule into these colonies:

For taking away our charters, abolishing our most valuable laws, and altering, fundamentally, the powers of our governments:

For suspending our own legislatures, and declaring themselves invested with power to legislate for us in all cases whatsoever.

He has abdicated government here, by declaring us out of his protection, and waging war against us.

He has plundered our seas, ravaged our coasts, burnt our towns, and destroyed the lives of our people.

He is, at this time, transporting large armies of foreign mercenaries to complete the works of death, desolation, and tyranny, already begun, with circumstances of cruelty and perfidy scarcely paralleled in the most barbarous ages, and totally unworthy the head of a civilized nation.

He has constrained our fellow-citizens, taken captive on the high seas, to bear arms against their country, to become the executioners of their friends and brethren, or to fall themselves by their hands.

He has excited domestic insurrections amongst us, and has endeavored to bring on the inhabitants of our frontiers, the merciless Indian savages, whose known rule of warfare is an undistinguished destruction, of all ages, sexes, and conditions.

In every stage of these oppressions, we have petitioned for redress, in the most humble terms; our repeated petitions have been answered only by repeated injury. A prince, whose character is thus marked by every act which may define a tyrant, is unfit to be the ruler of a free people.

Nor have we been wanting in attention to our British brethren. We have warned them, from time to time, of attempts made by their legislature to extend an unwarrantable jurisdiction over us. We have reminded them of the circumstances of our emigration and settlement here. We have appealed to their native justice and magnanimity, and we have conjured them, by the ties of our common kindred, to disavow these usurpations, which would inevitably interrupt our connections and correspondence. They, too, have been deaf to the voice of justice and consanguinity. We must, therefore, acquiesce in the necessity, which denounces our separation, and hold them, as we hold the rest of mankind, enemies in war, in peace, friends.

We, therefore, the representatives of the United States of America, in General Congress assembled, appealing to the Supreme Judge of the World for the rectitude of our intentions, do, in the name, and by the authority of the good people of these colonies, solemnly publish and declare, That these United Colonies are, and of right ought to be, free and independent States; that they are absolved from all allegiance to the British crown, and that all political connection between them and the state of Great Britain, is, and ought to be, totally dissolved; and that, as free and independent states, they have full power to levy war, conclude peace, contract alliances, establish commerce, and to do all other acts and things which independent States may of right do. And, for the support of this declaration, with a firm reliance on the protection of Divine Providence, we mutually pledge to each other, our lives, our fortunes, and our sacred honor.

The foregoing declaration was, by order of Congress, engrossed, and signed by the following members:—

JOHN HANCOCK.

New Hampshire.
Josiah Bartlett,
William Whipple,
Matthew Thornton.

Massachusetts Bay.
Samuel Adams,
John Adams,
Robert Treat Paine,
Elbridge Gerry.

Rhode Island.
Stephen Hopkins,
William Ellery.

Connecticut.
Roger Sherman,

Samuel Huntington,
William Williams,
Oliver Wolcott.

New York.
William Floyd,
Philip Livingston,
Francis Lewis,
Lewis Morris.

New Jersey.
Richard Stockton,
John Witherspoon,
Francis Hopkinson,
John Hart,
Abraham Clark.

Pennsylvania.
Robert Morris,
Benjamin Rush,
Benjamin Franklin,
John Morton,
George Clymer,
James Smith,
George Taylor,
James Wilson,
George Ross.

Delaware.
Cæsar Rodney,
George Read,
Thomas M'Kean.

Maryland.
Samuel Chase,
William Paca,
Thomas Stone,
Charles Carroll, of Carrollton.

Virginia.
George Wythe,
Richard Henry Lee,
Thomas Jefferson,
Benjamin Harrison,
Thomas Nelson, jr.,
Francis Lightfoot Lee,
Carter Braxton.

North Carolina.
William Hooper,
Joseph Hewes,
John Penn.

South Carolina.
Edward Rutledge,
Thomas Heyward, jr.,
Thomas Lynch, jr.,
Arthur Middleton.

Georgia.
Button Gwinnett,
Lyman Hall,
George Walton.

Resolved, That copies of the Declaration be sent to the several assemblies, conventions, and committees, or councils of safety, and to the several commanding officers of the continental troops; that it be proclaimed in each of the United States, and at the head of the army.

THE CONSTITUTION OF THE UNITED STATES.

We, the People of the United States, in order to form a more perfect union, establish justice, ensure domestic tranquillity, provide for the common defence, promote the general welfare, and secure the blessings of liberty to ourselves and our posterity, do ordain and establish this constitution for the United States of America.

ARTICLE I.
OF THE LEGISLATIVE POWER.

Sect. I. All legislative powers, herein granted, shall be vested in a congress of the United States, which shall consist of a senate and house of representatives.

Sect. II. 1. The house of representatives shall be composed of members chosen every second year by the people of the several states; and the electors in each state shall have the qualifications requisite for electors of the most numerous branch of the state legislature.

2. No person shall be a representative, who shall not have attained to the age of twenty-five years, and been seven years a citizen of the United States, and who shall not, when elected, be an inhabitant of that state in which he shall be chosen.

3. Representatives and direct taxes shall be apportioned among the several states which may be included within this union, according to their respective numbers, which shall be determined by adding to the whole number of free persons, including those bound to service for a term of years, and excluding Indians not taxed, three-fifths of all

other persons. The actual enumeration shall be made within three years after the first meeting of the congress of the United States, and within every subsequent term of ten years, in such manner as they shall by law direct. The number of representatives shall not exceed one for every thirty thousand, but each state shall have at least one representative; and, until such enumeration shall be made, the state of New Hampshire shall be entitled to choose three, Massachusetts eight, Rhode Island and Providence Plantations one, Connecticut five, New York six, New Jersey four, Pennsylvania eight, Delaware one, Maryland six, Virginia ten, North Carolina five, South Carolina five, and Georgia three.

4. When vacancies happen in the representation from any state, the executive authority thereof shall issue writs of election, to fill such vacancies.

5. The house of representatives shall choose their speaker and other officers; and shall have the sole power of impeachment.

SECT. III. 1. The senate of the United States shall be composed of two senators from each state, chosen by the legislature thereof for six years; and each senator shall have one vote.

2. Immediately after they shall be assembled, in consequence of the first election, they shall be divided, as equally as may be, into three classes. The seats of the senators of the first class shall be vacated at the expiration of the second year; of the second class at the expiration of the fourth year; and of the third class at the expiration of the sixth year; so that one-third may be chosen every second year. And if vacancies happen by resignation, or otherwise, during the recess of the legislature of any state, the executive thereof may make temporary appointments, until the next meeting of the legislature, which shall then fill such vacancies.

3. No person shall be a senator, who shall not have

attained to the age of thirty years, and been nine years a citizen of the United States, and who shall not, when elected, be an inhabitant of that state for which he shall be chosen.

4. The vice-president of the United States shall be president of the senate, but shall have no vote, unless they be equally divided.

5. The senate shall choose their other officers, and also a president pro tempore in the absence of the vice-president, or when he shall exercise the office of president of the United States.

6. The senate shall have the sole power to try all impeachments. When sitting for that purpose, they shall be on oath or affirmation. When the president of the United States is tried, the chief justice shall preside. And no person shall be convicted, without the concurrence of two-thirds of the members present.

7. Judgment in cases of impeachment shall not extend further than to removal from office, and disqualification to hold and enjoy any office of honor, trust or profit under the United States; but the party convicted shall, nevertheless, be liable and subject to indictment, trial, judgment and punishment, according to law.

SECT. IV. 1. The times, places, and manner of holding elections for senators and representatives, shall be prescribed in each state by the legislature thereof, but the congress may at any time, by law, make or alter such regulations, except as to the places of choosing senators.

2. Congress shall assemble at least once in every year, and such meeting shall be on the first Monday in December, unless they shall, by law, appoint a different day.

SECT. V. 1. Each house shall be the judge of the election returns and qualifications of its own members, and a majority of each shall constitute a quorum to do business, but a smaller number may adjourn from day to day, and may be authorized to compel the attendance of the absent members, in such manner, and under such penalties, as each house may provide.

2. Each house may determine the rules of its proceedings, punish its members for disorderly behavior, and with the concurrence of two-thirds, expel a member.

3. Each house shall keep a journal of its proceedings, and from time to time publish the same, excepting such parts as may in their judgment require secrecy; and the yeas and nays of members of either house on any question, shall, at the desire of one-fifth of those present, be entered on the journal.

4. Neither house, during the session of congress, shall, without the consent of the other, adjourn for more than three days, nor to any other place, than that in which the two houses shall be sitting.

Sect. VI. 1. The senators and representatives shall receive a compensation for their services, to be ascertained by law, and paid out of the treasury of the United States. They shall in all cases, except treason, felony and breach of the peace, be privileged from arrest during their attendance at the session of their respective houses, and in going to, and returning from the same; and for any speech or debate in either house, they shall not be questioned in any other place.

2. No senator or representative shall, during the time for which he was elected, be appointed to any civil office under the authority of the United States, which shall have been created, or the emoluments whereof shall have been increased, during such time; and no person holding any office under the United States, shall be a member of either house, during his continuance in office.

Sect. VII. 1. All bills for raising revenue shall originate in the house of representatives; but the senate may propose or concur with amendments, as on other bills.

2. Every bill which shall have passed the house of representatives and the senate, shall, before it become a law,

be presented to the president of the United States; if he approve, he shall sign it; but if not, he shall return it, with his objections, to that house in which it shall have originated, who shall enter the objections at large on their journal, and proceed to re-consider it. If, after such reconsideration, two-thirds of that house shall agree to pass the bill, it shall be sent, together with the objections, to the other house, by which it shall likewise be re-considered, and, if approved by two-thirds of that house, it shall become a law. But in all such cases, the votes of both houses shall be determined by yeas and nays, and the names of the persons voting for and against the bill shall be entered on the journal of each house, respectively. If any bill shall not be returned by the president within ten days (Sundays excepted) after it shall have been presented to him, the same shall be a law in like manner as if he had signed it, unless congress, by their adjournment, prevent its return, in which case it shall not be a law.

3. Every order, resolution or vote, to which the concurrence of the senate and house of representatives may be necessary (except on a question of adjournment), shall be presented to the president of the United States, and before the same shall take effect, shall be approved by him, or being disapproved by him, shall be re-passed by two-thirds of the senate and house of representatives, according to the rules and limitations prescribed in the case of a bill.

SECT. VIII. Congress shall have power—

1. To lay and collect taxes, duties, imposts and excises, to pay the debts, and provide for the common defence and general welfare of the United States; but all duties, imposts and excises, shall be uniform throughout the United States;

2. To borrow money on the credit of the United States;

3. To regulate commerce with foreign nations, and among the several states, and with the Indian tribes;

4. To establish a uniform rule of naturalization, and uni-

form laws on the subject of bankruptcies throughout the United States;

5. To coin money, regulate the value thereof, and of foreign coin, and fix the standard of weights and measures;

6. To provide for the punishment of counterfeiting the securities and current coin of the United States;

7. To establish post-offices and post-roads;

8. To promote the progress of science and useful arts, by securing, for limited times, to authors and inventors, the exclusive right to their respective writings and discoveries;

9. To constitute tribunals inferior to the supreme court;

10. To define and punish piracies, felonies committed on the high seas, and offences against the law of nations;

11. To declare war, grant letters of marque and reprisal, and make rules concerning captures on land and water;

12. To raise and support armies; but no appropriation of money to that use shall be for a longer term than two years;

13. To provide and maintain a navy;

14. To make rules for the government and regulation of the land and naval forces;

15. To provide for calling forth the militia to execute the laws of the Union, suppress insurrections, and repel invasions;

16. To provide for organizing, arming and disciplining the militia, and for governing such part of them as may be employed in the service of the United States, reserving to the states, respectively, the appointment of the officers, and the authority of training the militia, according to the discipline prescribed by congress;

18. To exercise exclusive legislation, in all cases whatsoever, over such district (not exceeding ten miles square) as may, by cession of particular states, and the acceptance of congress, become the seat of the government of the United States; and to exercise like authority over all places, pur-

chased by the consent of the legislature of the state in which the same shall be, for the erection of forts, magazines, arsenals, dockyards, and other needful buildings;

18. And to make all laws which shall be necessary and proper, for carrying into execution the foregoing powers, and all other powers vested by this constitution in the government of the United States, or in any department or officer thereof.

SECT. IX. 1. The migration or importation of such persons, as any of the states now existing shall think proper to admit, shall not be prohibited by congress, prior to the year one thousand eight hundred and eight; but a tax or duty may be imposed on such importation, not exceeding ten dollars for each person.

2. The privilege of the writ of *habeas corpus* shall not be suspended, unless when in cases of rebellion or invasion, the public safety may require it.

3. No bill of attainder, or *ex post facto* law shall be passed.

4. No capitation, or other direct tax, shall be laid, unless in proportion to the census or enumeration, hereinbefore directed to be taken.

5. No tax or duty shall be laid on articles exported from any state. No preference shall be given by any regulation of commerce or revenue, to the ports of one state over those of another; nor shall vessels bound to or from one state be obliged to enter, clear or pay duties in another.

6. No money shall be drawn from the treasury, but in consequence of appropriations made by law; and a regular statement and account of the receipts and expenditures of all public money shall be published from time to time.

7. No title of nobility shall be granted by the United States; and no person, holding any office of profit or trust under them, shall, without the consent of congress, accept of any present, emolument, office, or title, of any kind whatever, from any king, prince, or foreign state.

Sect. X. 1. No state shall enter into any treaty, alliance or confederation; grant letters of marque and reprisal; coin money; emit bills of credit; make anything but gold and silver coin a tender in the payment of debts; pass any bill of attainder, *ex post facto* law, or law impairing the obligations of contracts; or grant any title of nobility.

2. No state shall, without the consent of congress, lay any imposts or duties on imports or exports, except what may be absolutely necessary for executing its inspection laws; and the nett produce of all duties and imposts, laid by any state on imports or exports, shall be for the use of the treasury of the United States; and all such laws shall be subject to the revision and control of congress. No state shall, without the consent of congress, lay any duty on tonnage, keep troops or ships of war in time of peace, enter into any agreement or compact with another state, or with a foreign power, or engage in war, unless actually invaded, or in such imminent danger as will not admit of delay.

ARTICLE II.

OF THE EXECUTIVE.

Sect. I. 1. The executive power shall be vested in a president of the United States of America. He shall hold his office during the term of four years, and, together with the vice-president, chosen for the same term, be elected as follows:

2. Each state shall appoint, in such manner as the legislature thereof may direct, a number of electors, equal to the whole number of senators and representatives to which the state may be entitled in congress; but no senator or representative, or person holding an office of trust or profit under the United States, shall be appointed an elector.

3. The electors shall meet in their respective states and vote, by ballot, for two persons, of whom one at least shall not be an inhabitant of the same state with themselves.

And they shall make a list of all the persons voted for, and of the number of votes for each; which list they shall sign and certify, and transmit, sealed, to the seat of the government of the United States, directed to the president of the senate. The president of the senate shall, in the presence of the senate and house of representatives, open all the certificates, and the votes shall then be counted. The person having the greatest number of votes shall be the president, if such number be a majority of the whole number of electors appointed; and if there be more than one who have such majority, and have an equal number of votes, then the house of representatives shall immediately choose, by ballot, one of them for president; and if no person have a majority, then, from the five highest on the list, the said house shall, in like manner, choose the president, but in choosing the president the votes shall be taken by states, the representation from each state having one vote: a quorum for this purpose shall consist of a member or members from two-thirds of the states, and a majority of all the states shall be necessary to a choice. In every case, after the choice of the president, the person having the greatest number of votes of the electors, shall be the vice-president. But if there should remain two or more, who have equal votes, the senate shall choose from them, by ballot, the vice-president.

4. Congress may determine the time of choosing the electors, and the day on which they shall give their votes, which day shall be the same throughout the United States.

5. No person, except a natural-born citizen, or a citizen of the United States at the time of the adoption of this constitution, shall be eligible to the office of president; neither shall any person be eligible to that office, who shall not have attained to the age of thirty-five years, and been fourteen years a resident within the United States.

6. In case of the removal of the president from office, or of his death, resignation, or inability to discharge the powers

and duties of the said office, the same shall devolve on the vice-president; and congress may, by law, provide for the case of removal, death, resignation, or inability, both of the president and vice-president, declaring what officer shall then act as president, and such officer shall act accordingly, until the disability be removed, or a president shall be elected.

7. The president shall, at stated times, receive for his services a compensation, which shall neither be increased nor diminished during the period for which he shall have been elected; and he shall not receive, within that period, any other emolument from the United States, or any of them.

8. Before he enter on the execution of his office, he shall take the following oath or affirmation:

"I do solemnly swear (or affirm) that I will faithfully execute the office of president of the United States, and will, to the best of my ability, preserve, protect, and defend the constitution of the United States."

SECT. II. 1. The president shall be commander-in-chief of the army and navy of the United States, and of the militia of the several states, when called into the actual service of the United States; he may require the opinion, in writing, of the principal officer in each of the executive departments, upon any subject relating to the duties of their respective offices; and he shall have power to grant reprieves and pardons for offences against the United States, except in cases of impeachment.

2. He shall have power, by and with the advice and consent of the senate, to make treaties, provided two-thirds of the senators present concur; and he shall nominate, and, by and with the advice and consent of the senate, shall appoint ambassadors, other public ministers and consuls, judges of the supreme court, and all other officers of the United States, whose appointments are not herein otherwise provided for, and which shall be established by law.

But congress may, by law, vest the appointment of such inferior officers as they think proper, in the president alone, in the courts of law, or in the heads of departments.

3. The president shall have power to fill up all vacancies that may happen during the recess of the senate, by granting commissions, which shall expire at the end of their next session.

SECT. III. He shall, from time to time, give to congress information of the state of the union, and recommend to their consideration such measures as he shall judge necessary and expedient; he may, on extraordinary occasions, convene both houses, or either of them, and in case of disagreement between them, with respect to the time of adjournment, he may adjourn them to such time as he shall think proper; he shall receive ambassadors, and other public ministers; he shall take care that the laws be faithfully executed, and shall commission all the officers of the United States.

SECT. IV. The president, vice-president and all civil officers of the United States, shall be removed from office on impeachment for, and conviction of treason, bribery, or other high crimes and misdemeanors.

ARTICLE III.

OF THE JUDICIARY.

SECT. I. The judicial power of the United States shall be vested in one supreme court, and in such inferior courts as congress may, from time to time, ordain and establish. The judges, both of the supreme and inferior courts, shall hold their offices during good behavior, and shall, at stated times, receive for their services a compensation, which shall not be diminished during their continuance in office.

SECT. II. 1. The judicial power shall extend to all cases in law and equity arising under this constitution, the laws of the United States, and treaties made, or which shall be made, under their authority; to all cases affecting ambassadors, other public ministers and consuls; to all cases of admiralty and maritime jurisdiction; to controversies to which the United States shall be a party; to controversies between two or more states, between a state and a citizen of another state, between citizens of different states, between citizens of the same state claiming lands under grants of different states, and between a state, or the citizens thereof, and foreign states, citizens or subjects.

2. In all cases affecting ambassadors, other public ministers and consuls, and those in which a state shall be a party, the supreme court shall have original jurisdiction. In all the other cases before mentioned, the supreme court shall have appellate jurisdiction, both as to law and fact, with such exceptions, and under such regulations, as congress shall make.

3. The trial of all crimes, except in cases of impeachment, shall be by jury; and such trials shall be held in the state where the said crime shall have been committed; but when not committed within any state, the trial shall be at such place or places as congress may by law have directed.

SECT. III. 1. Treason against the United States shall consist only in levying war against them, or in adhering to their enemies, giving them aid and comfort. No person shall be convicted of treason, unless on the testimony of two witnesses to the same overt act, or on confession in open court.

2. Congress shall have power to declare the punishment of treason, but no attainder of treason shall work corruption of blood, or forfeiture, except during the life of the person attainted.

ARTICLE IV.

OF STATE RECORDS.

SECT. I. Full faith and credit shall be given in each state to the public acts, records and judicial proceedings of every other state. And congress may, by general laws, prescribe the manner in which such acts, records, and proceedings shall be proved, and the effect thereof.

OF CITIZENSHIP.

SECT. II. 1. The citizens of each state shall be entitled to all privileges and immunities of citizens in the several states.

OF FUGITIVES FROM JUSTICE.

2. A person charged in any state with treason, felony or other crime, who shall flee from justice, and be found in another state, shall, on demand of the executive authority of the same state from which he fled, be delivered up, to be removed to the state having jurisdiction of the crime.

OF FUGITIVE SLAVES.

3. No person held to service or labor in one state, under the laws thereof, escaping into another, shall, in consequence of any law or regulation therein, be discharged from such service or labor, but shall be delivered up, on claim of the party to whom such service or labor may be due.

OF THE ADMISSION OF NEW STATES.

SECT. III. 1. New states may be admitted by congress into this Union; but no new state shall be formed or erected within the jurisdiction of any other state, nor any state be formed by the junction of two or more states, or parts of states, without the consent of the legislatures of the states concerned, as well as of congress.

OF TERRITORIES.

2. Congress shall have power to dispose of, and make all needful rules and regulations respecting the territory, or other property, belonging to the United States; and nothing in this constitution shall be so construed, as to prejudice any claims of the United States, or of any particular state.

OF STATE FORMS OF GOVERNMENT.

SECT. IV. The United States shall guaranty to every

state in this union a republican form of government, and shall protect each of them against invasion; and, on application of the legislature, or of the executive (when the legislature cannot be convened), against domestic violence.

ARTICLE V.

OF AMENDMENTS TO THE CONSTITUTION.

Congress, whenever two-thirds of both houses shall deem it necessary, shall propose amendments to this constitution, or on the application of the legislatures of two-thirds of the several states, shall call a convention for proposing amendments, which, in either case, shall be valid, to all intents and purposes, as part of this constitution, when ratified by the legislatures of three-fourths of the several states, or by conventions in three-fourths thereof, as the one or the other mode of ratification may be proposed by congress: *Provided*, That no amendments which may be made prior to the year one thousand eight hundred and eight, shall in any manner affect the first and fourth clauses in the ninth section of the first article; and that no state, without its consent, shall be deprived of its equal suffrage in the senate.

ARTICLE VI.

PUBLIC DEBT.

SECT. I. All debts contracted, and engagements entered into, before the adoption of this constitution, shall be as valid against the United States under this constitution, as under the confederation.

OF THE SUPREME LAW OF THE LAND.

SECT. II. This constitution, and the laws of the United States, which shall be made in pursuance thereof, and all treaties made, or which shall be made under the authority of the United States, shall be the supreme law of the land; and the judges in every state shall be bound thereby, any thing in the constitution or laws of any state to the contrary nothwithstanding.

OF THE CONSTITUTIONAL OATH AND A RELIGIOUS TEST.

SECT. III. The senators and representatives before mentioned, and the members of the several state legislatures, and all executive and judicial officers, both of the United States and of the several states, shall be bound, by oath or affirmation, to support this constitution; but no religious test shall ever be required as a qualification to any office, or public trust, under the United States.

ARTICLE VII.

The ratification of the conventions of nine states shall be sufficient for the establishment of this constitution, between the states so ratifying the same.

Done in convention by the unanimous consent of the states present, the seventeenth day of September, in the year of our Lord one thousand seven hundred and eighty-seven, and of the Independence of the United States of America the twelfth. In witness whereof, we have hereunto subscribed our names.

GEORGE WASHINGTON, *President,*
And Deputy from Virginia.

New Hampshire.
John Langdon,
Nicholas Gilman.

Massachusetts.
Nathaniel Gorham,
Rufus King.

Connecticut.
William Samuel Johnson,
Roger Sherman,

New York.
Alexander Hamilton.

New Jersey.
William Livingston,
David Brearly,
William Patterson,
Jonathan Dayton.

Delaware.
George Read,
Gunning Bedford, jr.
John Dickinson,
Richard Bassett,
Jacob Broom.

Maryland.
James M'Henry,
Daniel of St. Tho. Jenifer,
Daniel Carroll.

Virginia.
John Blair,
James Madison, jr.

North Carolina.
William Blount,
Richard Dobbs Spaight,
Hugh Williamson.

Pennsylvania.
Benjamin Franklin,
Thomas Mifflin,
Robert Morris,
George Clymer,

Thomas Fitzsimmons,
Jared Ingersoll,
James Wilson,
Gouverneur Morris.

South Carolina.
John Rutlege,
Charles Cotesworth Pinkney,
Charles Pinkney,
Pierce Butler.

Georgia.
William Few,
Abraham Baldwin.

Attest. William Jackson, Secretary.

AMENDMENTS.

The following articles proposed by Congress, in addition to, and amendment of the constitution of the United States, having been ratified by the legislatures of the requisite number of the states, are become a part of the constitution.

First Congress. First Session. March 4, 1789.

ART. I. Congress shall make no law respecting an establishment of religion, or prohibiting the free exercise thereof; or abridging the freedom of speech, or of the press; or the right of the people peaceably to assemble, and to petition the government for a redress of grievances.

ART. II. A well regulated militia being necessary to the security of a free state, the right of the people to keep and bear arms shall not be infringed.

ART. III. No soldier shall in time of peace be quartered in any house, without the consent of the owner, nor in time of war, but in a manner to be prescribed by law.

ART. IV. The right of the people to be secure in their persons, houses, papers, and effects, against unreasonable searches and seizures, shall not be violated; and no warrants shall issue, but upon probable cause supported by oath or affirmation, and particularly describing the place to be searched, and the persons or things to be seized.

Art. V. No person shall be held to answer for a capital or otherwise infamous crime, unless on a presentment or indictment of a grand jury, except in cases arising in the land or naval forces, or in the militia, when in actual service in time of war or public danger; nor shall any person be subject, for the same offence, to be twice put in jeopardy of life or limb; nor shall be compelled, in any criminal case, to be a witness against himself; nor be deprived of life, liberty, or property, without due process of law; nor shall private property be taken for public use, without just compensation.

Art. VI. In all criminal prosecutions, the accused shall enjoy the right to a speedy and public trial, by an impartial jury of the state and district wherein the crime shall have been committed, which district shall have been previously ascertained by law; and to be informed of the nature and cause of the accusation; to be confronted with the witnesses against him; to have compulsory process for obtaining witnesses in his favor; and to have the assistance of counsel for his defence.

Art. VII. In suits at common law, where the value in controversy shall exceed twenty dollars, the right of trial by jury shall be preserved; and no fact tried by a jury shall be otherwise re-examined in any court of the United States, than according to the rules of the common law.

Art. VIII. Excessive bail shall not be required, nor excessive fines imposed, nor cruel and unusual punishments inflicted.

Art. IX. The enumeration in the constitution of certain rights shall not be construed to deny or disparage others retained by the people.

Art. X. The powers not delegated to the United States by the constitution, nor prohibited by it to the states, are reserved to the states respectively, or to the people.

Third Congress. Second Session. December 2, 1793.

Art. XI. The judicial power of the United States shall not be construed to extend to any suit in law or equity, commenced or prosecuted against one of the United States by citizens of another state, or by citizens or subjects of any foreign state.

Eighth Congress. First Session. October 17, 1803.

Art. XII. The electors shall meet in their respective states, and vote by ballot, for president and vice-president; one of whom at least shall not be an inhabitant of the same state with themselves; they shall name in their ballots the person voted for as president, and in distinct ballots the person voted for as vice-president; and they shall make distinct lists of all persons voted for as president; and of all persons voted for as vice-president, and the number of votes for each; which lists they shall sign and certify, and transmit sealed, to the seat of government of the United States, directed to the president of the senate; the president of the senate shall, in the presence of the senate and house of representatives, open all the certificates, and the votes shall then be counted; the person having the greatest number of votes for president, shall be the president, if such number be a majority of the whole number of electors appointed. And if no person have such majority, then from the persons having the highest numbers, not exceeding three on the list of those voted for as president, the house of representatives shall choose immediately, by ballot, the president; but in choosing the president, the votes shall be taken by states, the representation from each state having one vote; a quorum for this purpose shall consist of a member or members from two-thirds of the states, and a majority of all the states shall be necessary to a choice; and if the house of representatives shall not choose a president, whenever the right of choice shall devolve upon them, before the fourth day of March next following, then the vice-president shall act as president, as in the case of the death or other constitutional disability of the president. The person having the greatest number of votes as vice-president, shall be the vice-president, if such number be a majority of the whole number of electors appointed; and if no person have a majority, then from the two highest numbers on the list, the senate shall choose the vice-president; a quorum for the purpose shall consist of two-thirds of the whole number of senators, and a majority of the whole number shall be necessary to a choice. But no person constitutionally ineligible to the office of president, shall be eligible to that of vice-president of the United States.

Congress having passed the following amendment, when ratified by three-fourths of the several states, it will be valid as a part of this Constitution.

ARTICLE XIII.

Sect. 1. Neither slavery nor involuntary servitude, except as a punishment for crime, whereof the party shall have been duly convicted, shall exist within the United States, or any place subject to their jurisdiction.

Sect. 2. Congress shall have power to enforce this article by appropriate legislation.

CORRESPONDENCE OF BISHOPS ASBURY AND COKE WITH PRESIDENT WASHINGTON.

[The Methodist Episcopal Church in the United States, early in her history, and early in the history of our Republic, showed a loyal bearing, which we think should characterize all Christian organizations, thus complying with the teachings of inspiration: "Let every soul be subject to the higher powers;" "Put them in mind to be subject to principalities and powers, to obey magistrates, to be ready to every good work." We now introduce to our readers the correspondence of the Bishops of the M. E. Church with General Washington shortly after his selection as President of the United States. *See* Bangs' History of the Methodist Episcopal Church, Vol. I.]

ADDRESS OF THE BISHOPS OF THE M. E. CHURCH TO GENERAL WASHINGTON, THE FIRST PRESIDENT OF THE UNITED STATES.

SIR: We, the Bishops of the M. E. Church, humbly beg leave, in the name of our society collectively in these United States, to express to you the warm feelings of our hearts, and our sincere congratulations on your appointment to the Presidentship of these states. We are conscious from the signal proofs you have already given, that you are a friend of mankind; and under this established idea, place as full confidence in your wisdom and integrity for the preservation of those civil and religious liberties which have been transmitted to us by the providence of God and the glorious revolution, as we believe ought to be reposed in man. We have received the most grateful satisfaction from the humble and entire dependence on the great Governor of the universe which you have repeatedly expressed, acknowledging Him the source of every blessing, and particularly of the most excellent constitution of these States, which is at present the admiration of the world, and may in future become its great exemplar for imitation; and hence we enjoy a holy expectation, that you will always prove a faithful and impartial patron of genuine, vital religion, the grand end of our creation and present probationary existence. And we promise you our fervent prayers to the Throne of Grace, that God Almighty may endue you with all the graces and gifts of his Holy Spirit, that he may enable you to fill up your important station to his glory, the good of his church, the happiness and prosperity of the United States, and the welfare of mankind.

Signed, in behalf of the Methodist Episcopal Church,
THOMAS COKE,
FRANCIS ASBURY.

THE REPLY OF PRESIDENT WASHINGTON TO THE BISHOPS OF THE M. E. CHURCH.

NEW YORK, May 29, 1789.

GENTLEMEN: I return to you individually, and through you to your Society collectively in the United States, my thanks for the demonstrations of affection and the expressions of joy, offered in their behalf on my late appointment. It shall be my endeavor to manifest the purity of my inclinations for promoting the happiness of mankind, as well as the sincerity of my desires to contribute whatever may be in my power toward the civil and religious liberties of the American people. In pursuing this line of conduct, I hope, by the assistance of Divine Providence, not altogether to disappoint the confidence which you have been pleased to repose in me. It always affords me satisfaction when I find a concurrence of sentiment and practice between all conscientious men, in acknowledgments of homage to the great Governor of the universe, and in professions of support to a just civil government. After mentioning that I trust the people of every denomination, who demean themselves as good citizens, will have occasion to be convinced that I shall always strive to prove a faithful and impartial patron of genuine vital religion—I must assure you in particular, that I take in the kindest part the promise you make of presenting your prayers at the Throne of Grace for me, and that I likewise implore the divine benediction on yourselves and your religious community.

GEORGE WASHINGTON.

FAREWELL ADDRESS

OF

GEORGE WASHINGTON, PRESIDENT, TO THE PEOPLE OF THE UNITED STATES, SEPTEMBER 17, 1796.

Friends and Fellow-Citizens:

THE period for a new election of a citizen to administer the Executive Government of the United States being not far distant, and the time actually arrived when your thoughts must be employed in designating the person who is to be clothed with that important trust, it appears to me proper, especially as it may conduce to a more distinct expression of the public voice, that I should now apprise you of the resolution I have formed, to decline being considered among the number of those out of whom a choice is to be made.

I beg you, at the same time, to do me the justice to be assured that this resolution has not been taken without a strict regard to all the considerations appertaining to the relation which binds a dutiful citizen to his country; and that, in withdrawing the tender of service, which silence, in my situation, might imply, I am influenced by no diminution of zeal for your future interest; no deficiency of grateful respect for your past kindness; but am supported by a full conviction that the step is compatible with both.

The acceptance of, and continuance hitherto in, the office to which your suffrages have twice called me, have been a uniform sacrifice of inclination to the opinion of duty, and to a deference for what appeared to be your desire. I constantly hoped that it would have been much earlier in my power, consistently with motives which I was not at liberty to disregard, to return to that retirement from which I had been reluctantly drawn. The strength of my inclination to do this, previous to the last election, had even led to the preparation of an address to declare it to you; but mature reflection on the then perplexed and critical posture of our affairs with foreign nations, and the unanimous advice of persons entitled to my confidence, impelled me to abandon the idea.

I rejoice that the state of your concerns, external as well as internal, no longer renders the pursuit of inclination incompatible with the sentiment of duty or propriety; and am persuaded, whatever partiality may be retained for my services, that, in the present circumstances of our country, you will not disapprove my determination to retire.

The impressions with which I first undertook the arduous trust were explained on the proper occasion. In the discharge of this trust, I will only say, that I have with good intentions contributed towards the organization and administration of the Government the best exertions of which a very fallible judgment was capable. Not unconscious in the outset of the inferiority of my qualifications, experience, in my own eyes—perhaps still more in the eyes of others—has strengthened the motives to diffidence of myself; and every day the increasing weight of years admonishes me, more and more, that the shade of retirement is as necessary to me as it will be welcome. Satisfied that if any circumstances have given peculiar value to my services, they were temporary, I have the consolation to believe that, while choice and prudence invite me to quit the political scene, patriotism does not forbid it.

In looking forward to the moment which is intended to terminate the career of my public life, my feelings do not permit me to suspend the deep acknowledgment of that debt of gratitude which I owe to my beloved country for the many honors it has conferred upon me; still more for the steadfast confidence with which it has supported me;

and for the opportunities I have thence enjoyed of manifesting my inviolable attachment, by services faithful and persevering, though in usefulness unequal to my zeal. If benefits have resulted to our country from these services, let it always be remembered to your praise, and as an instructive example in our annals, that, under circumstances in which the passions, agitated in every direction, were liable to mislead; amidst appearances sometimes dubious, vicissitudes of fortune often discouraging; in situations in which, not unfrequently, want of success has countenanced the spirit of criticism—the constancy of your support was the essential prop of the efforts, and a guarantee of the plans, by which they were effected. Profoundly penetrated with this idea, I shall carry it with me to my grave, as a strong incitement to unceasing vows, that Heaven may continue to you the choicest tokens of its beneficence; that your union and brotherly affection may be perpetual; that the free constitution, which is the work of your hands, may be sacredly maintained; that its administration, in every department, may be stamped with wisdom and virtue; that, in fine, the happiness of the people of these States, under the auspices of liberty, may be made complete, by so careful a preservation and so prudent a use of this blessing as will acquire to them the glory of recommending it to the applause, the affection, and the adoption of every nation which is yet a stranger to it.

Here, perhaps, I ought to stop; but a solicitude for your welfare, which cannot end but with my life, and the apprehension of danger natural to that solicitude, urge me, on an occasion like the present, to offer to your solemn contemplation, and to recommend to your frequent review, some sentiments, which are the result of much reflection, of no inconsiderable observation, and which appear to me all-important to the permanency of your felicity as a people. These will be afforded to you with the more freedom, as you can only see in them the disinterested warnings of a parting friend, who can possibly have no personal motive to bias his counsel; nor can I forget, as an encouragement to it, your indulgent reception of my sentiments on a former and not dissimilar occasion.

Interwoven as is the love of liberty with every ligament of your hearts, no recommendation of mine is necessary to fortify or confirm the attachment.

The unity of government, which constitutes you one people, is also now dear to you. It is justly so; for it is a main pillar in the edifice of your real independence—the support of your tranquillity at home, your peace abroad, of your safety, of your prosperity, of that very liberty which you so highly prize. But as it is easy to foresee that, from different causes and from different quarters, much pains will be taken, many artifices employed, to weaken in your minds the conviction of this truth; as this is the point in your political fortress against which the batteries of internal and external enemies will be most constantly and actively (though often covertly and insidiously) directed—it is of infinite moment that you should properly estimate the immense value of your national union to your collective and individual happiness; that you should cherish a cordial, habitual, and immovable attachment to it; accustoming yourselves to think and speak of it as of the palladium of your political safety and prosperity; watching for its preservation with jealous anxiety; discountenancing whatever may suggest even a suspicion that it can, in any event, be abandoned; and indignantly frowning upon the first dawning of every attempt to alienate any portion of our country from the rest, or to enfeeble the sacred ties which now link together the various parts.

For this you have every inducement of sympathy and interest. Citizens by birth or choice, of a common country, that country has a right to concentrate your affections. The name of *American*, which belongs to you in your national capacity, must always exalt the just pride of patriotism, more than any appellation derived from local discriminations. With slight shades of difference, you have the same religion, manners, habits, and political principles. You have, in a common cause, fought and triumphed together; the independence and liberty you possess are the work of joint counsels and joint efforts, of common dangers, sufferings, and successes.

But these considerations, however powerfully they address themselves to your sensibility, are greatly outweighed by those which apply more immediately to your interest; here every portion of our country finds the most commanding motives for carefully guarding and preserving the union of the whole.

The North, in an unrestrained intercourse with the South, protected by the equal laws of a common government, finds, in the productions of the latter, great additional resources of maritime and commercial enterprise, and precious materials of manufacturing industry. The South, in the same intercourse, benefiting by the agency of the North, sees its agriculture grow, and its commerce expand. Turning partly into its own channels the seamen of the North, it finds its particular navigation invigorated; and while it contributes, in different ways, to nourish and increase the general mass of the national navigation, it looks forward to the protection of a maritime strength to which itself is unequally adapted. The East, in like intercourse with the West, already finds, and in the progressive improvement of interior communication, by land and water, will more and more find, a valuable vent for the commodities which it brings from abroad, or manufactures at home. The West derives from the East supplies requisite to its growth and comfort; and what is perhaps of still greater consequence, it must, of necessity, owe the secure enjoyment of indispensable outlets for its own productions, to the weight, influence, and the future maritime strength of the Atlantic side of the Union, directed by an indissoluble community of interest as one nation. Any other tenure by which the West can hold this essential advantage, whether derived from its own separate strength, or from an apostate and unnatural connection with any foreign power, must be intrinsically precarious.

While, then, every part of our country thus feels an immediate and particular interest in union, all the parts combined cannot fail to find, in the united mass of means and efforts, greater strength, greater resource, proportionably greater security from external danger, a less frequent interruption of their peace by foreign nations; and what is of inestimable value, they must derive from union an exemption from those broils and wars between themselves, which so frequently afflict neighboring countries, not tied together by the same government; which their own rivalships alone would be sufficient to produce, but which opposite foreign alliances, attachments, and intrigues, would stimulate and imbitter. Hence, likewise, they will avoid the necessity of those overgrown military establishments, which, under any form of government, are inauspicious to liberty, and which are to be regarded as particularly hostile to republican liberty; in this sense it is that your union ought to be considered as a main prop of your liberty, and that the love of the one ought to endear to you the preservation of the other.

These considerations speak a persuasive language to every reflecting and virtuous mind, and exhibit the continuance of the Union as a primary object of patriotic desire. Is there a doubt, whether a common government can embrace so large a sphere? Let experience solve it. To listen to mere speculation, in such a case, were criminal. We are authorized to hope, that a proper organization of the whole, with the auxiliary agency of governments for the respective subdivisions, will afford a happy issue to the experiment. It is well worth a fair and full experiment. With such powerful and obvious motives to union, affecting all parts of our country, while experience shall not have demonstrated its impracticability, there will always be reason to distrust the patriotism of those, who, in any quarter, may endeavor to weaken its bands.

In contemplating the causes which may disturb our Union, it occurs, as a matter of serious concern, that any ground should have been furnished for characterizing parties by geographical discriminations—Northern and Southern—Atlantic and Western: whence designing men may endeavor to excite a belief that there is a real difference in local interests and views. One of the expedients of party to acquire influence within particular districts, is to misrepresent the opinions and aims of other districts. You cannot shield yourselves too much against the jealousies and heart-burnings which spring from these misrepresentations; they tend to render alien to each other those who ought to be bound together by fraternal affection. The inhabitants of our western country have lately had a useful lesson on this head; they have seen in the negotiation by the Executive and in the unanimous ratification by the Senate, of the treaty with Spain, and in the universal satisfaction at that event throughout the United States, a decisive proof how unfounded were the suspicions propagated among them, of a policy in the General Government, and in the Atlantic States, unfriendly to their interests in regard to the Mississippi: they have been witnesses to the formation of two treaties—that with Great Britain, and that with Spain, which secure to them everything they could desire in respect to our foreign relations, towards confirming their prosperity. Will it not be their wisdom to rely for the preservation of these advantages on the Union by which they were procured? Will they not henceforth be deaf to those advisers, if such there are, who would sever them from their brethren, and connect them with aliens?

To the efficacy and permanency of your Union, a government for the whole is indispensable. No alliance, however strict between the parts, can be an adequate substitute; they must inevitably experience the infractions and interruptions which all alliances, in all time, have experienced. Sensible of this momentous truth, you have improved upon your first essay, by the adoption of a Constitution of Government better calculated than your former for an intimate Union, and for the efficacious management of your common concerns. This Government, the offspring of our own choice, uninfluenced and unawed, adopted upon full investigation and mature deliberation, completely free in its principles, in the distribution of its powers, uniting security with energy, and containing within itself a provision for its own amendment, has a just claim to your confidence and your support. Respect for its authority, compliance with its laws, acquiescence in its measures, are duties enjoined by the fundamental maxims of true liberty. The bases of our political systems, is the right of the people to make and to alter their constitutions of Government: but the Constitution which at any time exists, till changed by an explicit and authentic act of the whole people, is sacredly obligatory upon all. The very idea of the power, and the right of the people to establish Government, pre-supposes the duty of every individual to obey the established Government.

All obstructions to the execution of the laws, all combinations and associations, under whatever plausible character, with the real design to direct, control, counteract, or awe the regular deliberation and action of the constituted authorities, are destructive to this fundamental principle, and of fatal tendency. They serve to organize faction, to give it an artificial and extraordinary force, to put in the place of the delegated will of the nation, the will of a party, often a small but artful and enterprising minority of the community; and, according to the alternate triumphs of different parties, to make the public administration the mirror of the ill-concerted and incongruous projects of faction, rather than the organ of consistent and wholesome plans, digested by common counsels, and modified by mutual interests.

However combinations or associations of the above description may now and then answer popular ends, they are likely, in the course of time and things, to become potent engines, by which cunning, ambitious, and unprincipled men, will be enabled to subvert the power of the people, and to usurp for themselves the reins of Government; destroying, afterwards, the very engines which had lifted them to unjust dominion.

Towards the preservation of your Government, and the permanency of your present happy state, it is requisite, not only that you steadily discountenance irregular oppositions to its acknowledged authority, but also that you resist with care the spirit of innovation upon its principles, however specious the pretexts. One method of assault may be to effect, in the forms of the Constitution, alterations which will impair the energy of the system, and thus to undermine what cannot be directly overthrown. In all the changes to which you may be invited, remember that time and habit are at least as necessary to fix the true character of governments as of other human institutions; that experience is the surest standard by which to test the real tendency of the existing constitution of a country; that facility in changes, upon the credit of mere hypothesis and opinion, exposes to perpetual change, from the endless variety of hypothesis and opinion; and remember, especially, that for the efficient management of your common interests, in a country so extensive as ours, a Government of as much vigor as is consistent with the perfect security of liberty, is indispensable. Liberty itself will find in such a Government, with powers properly distributed and adjusted, its surest guardian. It is, indeed, little else than a name, where the Government is too feeble to withstand the enterprises of faction, to confine each member of the society within the limits prescribed by the laws, and to maintain all in the secure and tranquil enjoyment of the rights of person and property.

I have already intimated to you the danger of parties in the State, with particular reference to the founding of them on geographical discriminations. Let me now take a more comprehensive view, and warn you, in the most solemn manner, against the baneful effects of the spirit of party generally.

This spirit, unfortunately, is inseparable from our nature, having its root in the strongest passions of the human mind. It exists under different shapes, in all governments, more or less stifled, controlled, or repressed; but in those of the popular form it is seen in its greatest rankness, and is truly their worst enemy.

The alternate domination of one faction over another, sharpened by the spirit of revenge, natural to party dissension, which, in different ages and countries, has perpetrated the most horrid enormities, is itself a frightful despotism. But this leads, at length, to a more formal and permanent despotism. The disorders and miseries which result, gradually incline the minds of men to seek security and repose in the absolute power of an individual; and, sooner or later, the chief of some prevailing faction, more able or more fortunate than his competitors, turns this disposition to the purposes of his own elevation on the ruins of public liberty.

Without looking forward to an extremity of this kind, (which, nevertheless, ought not to be entirely out of sight), the common and continual mischiefs of the spirit of party are sufficient to make it the interest and duty of a wise people to discourage and restrain it.

It serves always to distract the public councils, and enfeeble the public administration. It agitates the community with ill-founded jealousies and false alarms; kindles the animosity of one part against another; foments, occasionally, riot and insurrection. It opens the door to foreign influence and corruption, which find a facilitated access to the

Government itself, through the channels of party passions. Thus the policy and the will of one country are subjected to the policy and will of another.

There is an opinion that parties, in free countries, are useful checks upon the administration of the Government, and serve to keep alive the spirit of liberty. This, within certain limits, is probably true; and in Governments of a monarchical cast, patriotism may look with indulgence, if not with favor, upon the spirit of party. But in those of the popular character, in Governments purely elective, it is a spirit not to be encouraged. From their natural tendency, it is certain there will always be enough of that spirit for every salutary purpose. And there being constant danger of excess, the effort ought to be, by force of public opinion, to mitigate and assuage it. A fire not to be quenched, it demands a uniform vigilance to prevent its bursting into a flame, lest, instead of warming, it should consume.

It is important, likewise, that the habits of thinking, in a free country, should inspire caution in those intrusted with its administration, to confine themselves within their respective constitutional spheres, avoiding, in the exercise of the powers of one department, to encroach upon another. The spirit of encroachment tends to consolidate the powers of all the departments in one, and thus to create, whatever the form of Government, a real despotism. A just estimate of that love of power, and proneness to abuse it which predominates in the human heart, is sufficient to satisfy us of the truth of this position. The necessity of reciprocal checks in the exercise of political power, by dividing and distributing it into different depositories, and constituting each the guardian of the public weal, against invasions by the others, has been evinced by experiments, ancient and modern; some of them in our own country, and under our own eyes. To preserve them must be as necessary as to institute them. If, in the opinion of the people, the distribution or modification of the constitutional powers be, in any particular, wrong, let it be corrected by an amendment in the way which the Constitution designates. But let there be no change by usurpation; for though this, in one instance, may be the instrument of good, it is the customary weapon by which free Governments are destroyed. The precedent must always greatly overbalance, in permanent evil, any partial or transient benefit which the use can, at any time, yield.

Of all the dispositions and habits which lead to political prosperity, religion and morality are indispensable supports. In vain would that man claim the tribute of patriotism, who should labor to subvert these great pillars of human happiness, these firmest props of the duties of men and citizens. The mere politician, equally with the pious man, ought to respect and to cherish them. A volume could not trace all their connections with private and public felicity. Let it simply be asked, where is the security for property, for reputation, for life, if the sense of religious obligation *desert* the oaths which are the instruments of investigation in courts of justice? And let us with caution indulge the supposition, that morality can be maintained without religion. Whatever may be conceded to the influence of refined education on minds of peculiar structure, reason and experience both forbid us to expect that national morality can prevail in exclusion of religious principles.

It is substantially true, that virtue or morality is a necessary spring of popular Government. The rule, indeed, extends with more or less force to every species of free Government. Who, that is a sincere friend to it, can look with indifference upon attempts to shake the foundation of the fabric?

Promote, then, as an object of primary importance, institutions, for the general diffusion of knowledge. In proportion as the structure of a Government gives force to public opinion, it is essential that public opinion should be enlightened.

As a very important source of strength and security, cherish public credit. One method of preserving it is to use it as sparingly as possible; avoiding occasions of expense by cultivating peace, but remembering also that timely disbursements to prepare for danger, frequently prevent much greater disbursements to repel it; avoiding, likewise, the accumulation of debt, not only by shunning occasions of expense, but by vigorous exertions in time of peace to discharge the debts which unavoidable wars may have occasioned; not ungenerously throwing upon posterity the burden which we ourselves ought to bear. The execution of these maxims belongs to your representatives, but it is necessary that public opinion should co-operate. To facilitate to them the performance of their duty, it is essential that you should practically bear in mind, that towards the payment of debts there must be revenue; that to have revenue there must be taxes; that no taxes can be devised, which are not more or less inconvenient and unpleasant; that the intrinsic embarrassment inseparable from the selection of the proper objects (which is always a choice of difficulties), ought to be a decisive motive for a candid construction of the conduct of the Government in making it, and for a spirit of acquiescence in the measures for obtaining revenue, which the public exigencies may at any time dictate.

Observe good faith and justice towards all nations; cultivate peace and harmony with all; religion and morality enjoin this conduct; and can it be that good policy does not equally enjoin it? It will be worthy of a free, enlightened, and, at no distant period, a great nation, to give to mankind the magnanimous and too novel example of a people always guided by an exalted justice and benevolence. Who can doubt that, in the course of time and things, the fruits of such a plan would richly repay any temporary advantages which might be lost by a steady adherence to it? Can it be that Providence has not connected the permanent felicity of a nation with its virtue? The experiment, at least, is recommended by every sentiment which ennobles human nature. Alas! it is rendered impossible by its vices?

In the execution of such a plan, nothing is more essential than that permanent inveterate antipathies against particular nations, and passionate attachments for others, should be excluded; and that, in place of them, just and amicable feelings toward all should be cultivated. The nation which indulges towards another an habitual hatred, or an habitual fondness, is, in some degree, a slave. It is a slave to its animosity or to its affection; either of which is sufficient to lead it astray from its duty and its interest. Antipathy in one nation against another, disposes each more readily to offer insult and injury, to lay hold of slight causes of umbrage, and to be haughty and intractable, when accidental or trifling occasions of dispute occur. Hence frequent collisions, obstinate, envenomed, and bloody contests. The nation, prompted by ill will and resentment, sometimes impels to war the Government, contrary to the best calculations of policy. The Government sometimes participates in the national propensity, and adopts, through passion, what reason would reject; at other times it makes the animosity of the nation subservient to projects of hostility, instigated by pride, ambition, and other sinister and pernicious motives. The peace often, sometimes perhaps the liberty, of nations has been the victim.

So, likewise, a passionate attachment of one nation to another produces a variety of evils. Sympathy for the favorite nation, facilitating the illusion of an imaginary common interest, in cases where no real common interest exists, and infusing into one the enmities of the other, betrays the former into a participation in the quarrels and wars of the latter, without adequate inducement or justification. It leads also to concessions to the favorite nation of privileges denied to others, which is apt doubly to injure the nation making the concessions; by unnecessarily parting with what ought to have been retained, and by exciting jealousy, ill will, and a disposition to retaliate, in the parties from whom equal privileges are withheld; and it gives to ambitious, corrupted, or deluded citizens (who devote themselves to the favorite nation) facility to betray, or sacrifice the interest of their own country, without odium; sometimes even with popularity; gilding with the appearance of a virtuous sense of obligation, a commendable deference for public opinion, or a laudable zeal for public good, the base or foolish compliances of ambition, corruption, or infatuation.

As avenues to foreign influence in innumerable ways, such attachments are particularly alarming to the truly enlightened and independent patriot. How many opportunities do they afford to tamper with domestic factions, to practise the art of seduction, to mislead public opinion, to influence or awe the public councils! Such an attachment of a small or weak, towards a great and powerful nation, dooms the former to be the satellite of the latter.

Against the insidious wiles of foreign influence (I conjure you to believe me, fellow-citizens) the jealousy of a free people ought to be *constantly* awake; since history and experience prove that foreign influence is one of the most baneful foes of republican Government. But that jealousy, to be useful, must be impartial; else it becomes the instrument of the very influence to be avoided, instead of a defence against it. Excessive partiality for one foreign nation, and excessive dislike for another, cause those whom they actuate to see danger only on one side, and serve to veil, and even second, the arts of influence on the other. Real patriots, who may resist the intrigues of the favorite, are liable to become suspected and odious; while its tools and dupes usurp the applause and confidence of the people, to surrender their interests.

The great rule of conduct for us, in regard to foreign nations, is, in extending our commercial relations, to have with them as little political connection as possible. So far as we have already formed engagements, let them be fulfilled with perfect good faith. Here let us stop.

Europe has a set of primary interests, which to us have none, or a very remote relation. Hence she must be engaged in frequent controversies, the causes of which are essentially foreign to our concerns. Hence, therefore, it must be unwise in us to implicate ourselves, by artificial ties, in the ordinary vicissitudes of her politics, or the ordinary combinations and collisions of her friendships or enmities.

Our detached and distant situation invites and enables us to pursue a different course. If we remain one people, under an efficient Government, the period is not far off when we may defy material injury from external annoyance; when we may take such an attitude as will cause the neutrality we may at any time resolve upon, to be scrupulously respected; when belligerent nations, under the impossibility of making acquisitions upon us, will not lightly hazard the giving us provocation; when we may choose peace or war, as our interest, guided by justice, shall counsel.

Why forego the advantages of so peculiar a situation? Why quit our own to stand upon foreign ground? Why, by interweaving our destiny with that of any part of Europe, entangle our peace and prosperity in the toils of European ambition, rivalship, interest, humor, or caprice?

It is our true policy to steer clear of permanent alliances with any portion of the foreign world; so far, I mean, as we are now at liberty to do it; for let me not be understood as capable of patronizing infidelity to existing engagements. I hold the maxim no less applicable to public than to private affairs, that honesty is always the best policy. I repeat it, therefore, let those engagements be observed in their genuine sense. But, in my opinion, it is unnecessary and would be unwise to extend them.

Taking care always to keep ourselves, by suitable establishments, on a respectable defensive posture, we may safely trust to temporary alliances for extraordinary emergencies.

Harmony, and a liberal intercourse with all nations, are recommended by policy, humanity, and interest. But even our commercial policy should hold an equal and impartial hand; neither seeking nor granting exclusive favors or preferences; consulting the natural course of things; diffusing and diversifying, by gentle means, the streams of commerce, but forcing nothing; establishing, with powers so disposed, in order to give trade a stable course, to define the rights of our merchants, and to enable the Government to support them, conventional rules of intercourse, the best that present circumstances and mutual opinions will permit, but temporary, and liable to be, from time to time, abandoned or varied, as experience and circumstances shall dictate; constantly keeping in view, that it is folly in one nation to look for disinterested favors from another; that it must pay, with a portion of its independence, for whatever it may accept under that character; that by such acceptance it may place itself in the condition of having given equivalents for nominal favors, and yet of being reproached with ingratitude for not giving more. There can be no greater error than to expect, or calculate upon, real favors from nation to nation. It is an illusion which experience must cure, which a just pride ought to discard.

In offering to you, my countrymen, these counsels of an old and affectionate friend, I dare not hope they will make the strong and lasting impression I could wish; that they will control the usual current of the passions, or prevent our nation from running the course which has hitherto marked the destiny of nations; but if I may even flatter myself that they may be productive of some partial benefit, some occasional good; that they may now and then recur to moderate the fury of party spirit, to warn against the mischiefs of foreign intrigues, to guard against the impostures of pretended patriotism; this hope will be a full recompense for the solicitude for your welfare by which they have been dictated.

How far, in the discharge of my official duties, I have been guided by the principles which have been delineated, the public records, and other evidences of my conduct, must witness to you and the world. To myself, the assurance of my own conscience is, that I have at least believed myself to be guided by them.

In relation to the still subsisting war in Europe, my proclamation of the 22d of April, 1793, is the index to my plan. Sanctioned by your approving voice, and by that of your Representatives in both Houses of Congress, the spirit of that measure has continually governed me, uninfluenced by any attempts to deter or divert me from it.

After deliberate examination, with the aid of the best lights I could obtain, I was well satisfied that our country, under all the circumstances of the case, had a right to take, and was bound in duty and interest to take, a neutral position. Having taken it I determined, as far as should depend upon me, to maintain it with moderation, perseverance, and firmness.

The considerations which respect the right to hold this conduct, it is not necessary on this occasion to detail. I will only observe, that, according to my understanding of the matter, that right, so far from being denied by any of the belligerent powers, has been virtually admitted by all.

The duty of holding a neutral conduct may be inferred, without anything more, from the obligation which justice and humanity impose on every nation, in cases in which it is free to act, to maintain inviolate the relations of peace and amity towards other nations.

The inducements of interest, for observing that conduct, will best be referred to your own reflections and experience. With me, a predominant, motive has been to endeavor to gain time to our country to settle and mature its yet recent institutions, and to progress, without interruption, to that degree of strength and consistency which is necessary to give it, humanly speaking, the command of its own fortunes.

Though in reviewing the incidents of my administration, I am unconscious of intentional error; I am, nevertheless, too sensible of my defects not to think it probable that I may have committed many errors. Whatever they may be, I fervently beseech the Almighty to avert or mitigate the evils to which they may tend. I shall also carry with me the hope, that my country will never cease to view them with indulgence; and that, after forty-five years of my life dedicated to its service with an upright zeal, the faults of incompetent abilities will be consigned to oblivion, as myself must soon be to the mansions of rest.

Relying on its kindness in this, as in other things, and actuated by that fervent love towards it which is so natural to a man who views in it the native soil of himself and his progenitors for several generations, I anticipate, with pleasing expectation, that retreat in which I promise myself to realize, without alloy, the sweet enjoyment of partaking, in the midst of my fellow-citizens, the benign influence of good laws under a free Government—the ever favorite object of my heart—and the happy reward, as I trust, of our mutual cares, labors, and dangers.

GEORGE WASHINGTON.

United States, 17th September, 1796.

RECEPTION OF MR. LINCOLN IN PHILADELPHIA—INDEPENDENCE HALL.

Mr. Lincoln's reception in Philadelphia en route for Washington to take his seat as President, was exceedingly cordial on the part of the municipal authorities, and indeed the people generally were delighted to see the President elect, of whom they had only known and heard "by the hearing of the ear." On the morning of the 22d of February, 1861, he visited the old Independence Hall, for the purpose of raising the national flag over it. There he was received with a warm welcome, and made the following address:—

"I am filled with deep emotion at finding myself standing here, in this place, where were collected the wisdom, the patriotism, the devotion to principle, from which sprang the institutions under which we live. You have kindly suggested to me that in my hands is the task of restoring peace to the present distracted condition of the country. I can say in return, sir, that all the political sentiments I entertain have been drawn, so far as I have been able to draw them, from the sentiments which originated and were given to the world from this hall. I have never had a feeling politically that did not spring from the sentiments embodied in the Declaration of Independence. I have often pondered over the dangers which were incurred by the men who assembled here, and framed and adopted that Declaration of Independence. I have pondered over the toils that were endured by the officers and soldiers of the army who achieved that independence. I have often inquired of myself what great principle or idea it was that kept this Confederacy so long together. It was not the mere matter of the separation of the colonies from the mother-land, but that sentiment in the Declaration of Independence which gave liberty, not alone to the people of this country, but, I hope, to the world for all future time. It was that which gave promise that in due time the weight would be lifted from the shoulders of all men. This is a sentiment embodied in the Declaration of Independence. Now, my friends, can this country be saved upon this basis? If it can, I will consider myself one of the happiest men in the world if I can help to save it. If it cannot be saved upon that principle, it will be truly awful. But if this country cannot be saved without giving up that principle, *I was about to say I would rather be assassinated on this spot than surrender it.* Now, in my view of the present aspect of affairs, there need be no bloodshed or war. There is no necessity for it. I am not in favor of such a course, and I may say, in advance, that there will be no blood shed unless it be forced upon the government, and then it will be compelled to act in self-defence.

"My friends, this is wholly an unexpected speech, and I did not expect to be called upon to say a word when I came here. I supposed it was merely to do something towards raising the flag. I may, therefore, have said something indiscreet. I have said nothing but what I am willing to live by, and, if it be the pleasure of Almighty God, to die by."

At the platform in front of the State House, Mr. Benton, of the Select Council, invited the President elect to raise the flag. Mr. Lincoln responded in a brief speech, stating his cheerful compliance with the request, and alluded to the original flag of thirteen stars, saying that the number had increased as time rolled on, and we became a happy and powerful people, each star adding to its prosperity. "The future," he added, "is in the hands of the people. It is on such an occasion as this that we can reason together, reaffirm our devotion to the country and the principles of the Declaration of Independence. Let us make up our mind, that when we do put a new star upon our banner it shall be a fixed one, never to be dimmed by the horrors of war, but brightened by the contentment and prosperity of peace. Let us go on to extend the area of our usefulness, add star upon star, until their light shall shine upon five hundred millions of free and happy people." The President elect then raised the starry banner to the top of the staff, amid the long and loud cheering of a delighted people.

FIRST INAUGURAL ADDRESS OF ABRAHAM LINCOLN.

"FELLOW-CITIZENS OF THE UNITED STATES: In compliance with a custom as old as the Government itself, I appear before you to address you briefly, and to take, in your presence, the oath prescribed by the Constitution of the United States to be taken by the President before he enters on the execution of his office.

"I do not consider it necessary, at present, for me to discuss those matters of administration about which there is no special anxiety or excitement. Apprehension seems to exist among the people of the Southern States, that, by the accession of a Republican Administration, their property and their peace and personal security are to be endangered. There has never been any reasonable cause for such apprehension. Indeed, the most ample evidence to the contrary has all the while existed, and been open to their inspection. It is found in nearly all the published speeches of him who now addresses you. I do but quote from one of those speeches, when I declare that 'I have no purpose, directly or indirectly, to interfere with the institution of slavery in the States where it exists.' I believe I have no lawful right to do so; and I have no inclination to do so. Those who nominated and elected me, did so with the full knowledge that I had made this, and made many similar declarations, and had never recanted them. And, more than this, they placed in the platform, for my acceptance, and as a law to themselves and to me, the clear and emphatic resolution which I now read:—

"'*Resolved*, That the maintenance inviolate of the rights

of the States, and especially the right of each State to order and control its own domestic institutions according to its own judgment exclusively, is essential to that balance of power on which the perfection and endurance of our political fabric depend; and we denounce the lawless invasion, by armed force, of the soil of any State or Territory, no matter under what pretext, as among the gravest of crimes.'

"I now reiterate these sentiments; and in doing so, I only press upon the public attention the most conclusive evidence of which the case is susceptible, that the property, peace and security of no section are to be in anywise endangered by the now incoming administration.

"I add, too, that all the protection which, consistently with the Constitution and the laws, can be given, will be cheerfully given to all the States when lawfully demanded, for whatever cause, as cheerfully to one section as to another.

"There is much controversy about the delivering up of fugitives from service or labor. The clause I now read is as plainly written in the Constitution as any other of its provisions:—

"'No person held to service or labor in one State under the laws thereof, escaping into another, shall, in consequence of any law or regulation therein, be discharged from such service or labor, but shall be delivered up on claim of the party to whom such service or labor may be due.'

"It is scarcely questioned that this provision was intended by those who made it for the reclaiming of what we call fugitive slaves; and the intention of the lawgiver is the law.

"All members of Congress swear their support to the whole Constitution—to this provision as well as any other. To the proposition, then, that slaves whose cases come within the terms of this clause 'shall be delivered up,' their oaths are unanimous. Now, if they would make the effort in good temper, could they not, with nearly equal unanimity, frame and pass a law by means of which to keep good that unanimous oath?

"There is some difference of opinion whether this clause should be enforced by National or by State authority; but surely that difference is not a very material one. If the slave is to be surrendered, it can be of but little consequence to him or to others by which authority it is done; and should any one, in any case, be content that this oath shall go unkept on a merely unsubstantial controversy as to how it shall be kept?

"Again, in any law upon this subject, ought not all the safeguards of liberty known in civilized and humane jurisprudence to be introduced, so that a free man be not, in any case, surrendered as a slave? And might it not be well at the same time to provide by law for the enforcement of that clause in the Constitution which guarantees that 'the citizens of each State shall be entitled to all the privileges and immunities of citizens in the several States?'

"I take the official oath to day with no mental reservations, and with no purpose to construe the Constitution or laws by any hypercritical rules; and while I do not choose now to specify particular acts of Congress as proper to be enforced, I do suggest that it will be much safer for all, both in official and private stations, to conform to and abide by all those acts which stand unrepealed, than to violate any of them, trusting to find impunity in having them held to be unconstitutional.

"It is seventy-two years since the first inauguration of a President under our National Constitution. During that period, fifteen different and very distinguished citizens have in succession administered the executive branch of the Government. They have conducted it through many perils, and generally with great success. Yet, with all this scope for precedent, I now enter upon the same task, for the brief constitutional term of four years, under great and peculiar difficulties.

"A disruption of the Federal Union, heretofore only menaced, is now formidably attempted. I hold that in the contemplation of universal law and of the Constitution, the Union of these States is perpetual. Perpetuity is implied, if not expressed, in the fundamental law of all national governments. It is safe to assert that no government proper ever had a provision in its organic law for its own termination. Continue to execute all the express provisions of our National Constitution, and the Union will endure forever, it being impossible to destroy it, except by some action not provided for in the instrument itself.

"Again, if the United States be not a government proper, but an association of States in the nature of a contract merely, can it, as a contract, be peaceably unmade by less than all the parties who made it? One party to a contract may violate it—break it, so to speak; but does it not require to all lawfully rescind it? Descending from these general principles, we find the proposition that in legal contemplation the Union is perpetual, confirmed by the history of the Union itself.

"The Union is much older than the Constitution. It was formed, in fact, by the Articles of Association in 1774. It was matured and continued in the Declaration of Independence in 1776. It was further matured, and the faith of all the then thirteen States expressly plighted and engaged that it should be perpetual, by the Articles of the Confederation, in 1778; and finally, in 1787, one of the declared objects for ordaining and establishing the Constitution was to form a more perfect Union. But if the destruction of the Union by one or by a part only of the States be lawfully possible, the Union is less than before, the Constitution having lost the vital element of perpetuity.

"It follows from these views that no State, upon its own mere motion, can lawfully get out of the Union; that resolves and ordinances to that effect, are legally void; and that acts of violence within any State or States against the authority of the United States, are insurrectionary or revolutionary, according to circumstances.

"I therefore consider that, in view of the Constitution and the laws, the Union is unbroken, and, to the extent of my ability, I shall take care, as the Constitution itself expressly enjoins upon me, that the laws of the Union shall be faithfully executed in all the States. Doing this, which I deem to be only a simple duty on my part, I shall perfectly perform it, so far as is practicable, unless my rightful masters, the American people, shall withold the requisition, or in some authoritative manner direct the contrary.

"I trust this will not be regarded as a menace, but only as the declared purpose of the Union that it will constitutionally defend and maintain itself.

"In doing this there need be no bloodshed or violence, and there shall be none unless it is forced upon the National authority.

"The power confided to me *will be used to hold, occupy, and possess the property and places belonging to the Government*, and collect the duties and imposts; but beyond what may be necessary for these objects there will be no invasion, no using of force against or among the people anywhere.

"Where hostility to the United States shall be so great and so universal as to prevent competent resident citizens from holding Federal offices, there will be no attempt to force obnoxious strangers among the people that object. While the strict legal right may exist of the Government to enforce the exercise of these offices, the attempt to do so would be so irritating, and so nearly impracticable withal, that I deem it best to forego, for the time, the uses of such offices.

"The mails, unless repelled, will continue to be furnished in all parts of the Union.

"So far as possible, the people everywhere shall have that sense of perfect security which is most favorable to calm thought and reflection.

"The course here indicated will be followed, unless current events and experience shall show a modification or change to be proper; and in every case and exigency my best discretion will be exercised according to the circumstances actually existing, and with a view and hope of a peaceful solution of the National troubles, and the restoration of fraternal sympathies and affections.

"That there are persons, in one section or another, who seek to destroy the Union at all events, and are glad of any pretext to do it, I will neither affirm nor deny. But if there be such, I need address no word to them.

"To those, however, who really love the Union, may I not speak, before entering upon so grave a matter as the destruction of our National fabric, with all its benefits, its memories, and its hopes? Would it not be well to ascertain why we do it? Will you hazard so desperate a step, while any portion of the ills you fly from have no real existence? Will you, while the certain ills you fly to are greater than all the real ones you fly from? Will you risk the commission of so fearful a mistake? All profess to be content in the Union if all constitutional rights can be maintained. Is it true, then, that any right, plainly written in the Constitution, has been denied? I think not. Happily the human mind is so constituted, that no party can reach to the audacity of doing this.

"Think, if you can, of a single instance in which a plainly-written provision of the Constitution has ever been denied. If, by the mere force of numbers, a majority should deprive a minority of any clearly-written constitutional right, it might, in a moral point of view, justify revolution; it certainly would, if such right were a vital one. But such is not our case.

"All the vital rights of minorities and of individuals are so plainly assured to them by affirmations and negations, guaranties and prohibitions in the Constitution, that controversies never arise concerning them. But no organic law can ever be framed with a provision specifically applicable to every question which may occur in practical administration. No foresight can anticipate, nor any document of reasonable length contain, express provisions for all possible questions. Shall fugitives from labor be surrendered by National or by State authorities? The Constitution does not expressly say. Must Congress protect slavery in the Territories? The Constitution does not expressly say. From questions of this class, spring all our constitutional controversies, and we divide upon them into majorities and minorities.

"If the minority will not acquiesce, the majority must, or the Government must cease. There is no alternative for continuing the Government but acquiescence on the one side or the other. If a minority in such a case will secede rather than acquiesce, they make a precedent which, in turn, will ruin and divide them, for a minority of their own will secede from them whenever a majority refuses to be controlled by such a minority. For instance, why not any portion of a new Confederacy, a year or two hence, arbitrarily secede again, precisely as portions of the present Union now claim to secede from it? All who cherish disunion sentiments are now being educated to the exact temper of doing this. Is there such perfect identity of interests among the States to compose a new Union as to produce harmony only, and prevent renewed secession? Plainly, the central idea of secession is the essence of anarchy.

"A majority held in restraint by constitutional check and limitation, and always changing easily with deliberate changes of popular opinions and sentiments, is the only true sovereign of a free people. Whoever rejects it, does, of necessity, fly to anarchy or to despotism. Unanimity is impossible; the rule of a majority, as a permanent arrangement, is wholly inadmissible. So that, rejecting the majority principle, anarchy or despotism, in some form, is all that is left.

"I do not forget the position assumed by some that constitutional questions are to be decided by the Supreme Court, nor do I deny that such decisions must be binding in any case upon the parties to a suit, as to the object of that suit, while they are also entitled to a very high respect and consideration in all parallel cases by all other departments of the Government; and while it is obviously possible that such decision may be erroneous in any given case, still the evil effect following it, being limited to that particular case, with the chance that it may be overruled and never become a precedent for other cases, can better be borne than could the evils of a different practice.

"At the same time the candid citizen must confess that if the policy of the Government upon the vital question affecting the whole people is to be irrevocably fixed by the decisions of the Supreme Court, the instant they are made, as in ordinary litigation between parties in personal actions, the people will have ceased to be their own masters, unless having to that extent practically resigned their Government into the hands of that eminent tribunal.

"Nor is there in this view any assault upon the Court or the Judges. It is a duty from which they may not shrink, to decide cases properly brought before them; and it is no fault of theirs if others seek to turn their decisions to political purposes. One section of our country believes slavery is right and ought to be extended, while the other believes it is wrong and ought not to be extended; and this is the only substantial dispute; and the fugitive slave clause of the Constitution, and the law for the suppression of the foreign slave-trade, are each as well enforced, perhaps, as any law can ever be in a community where the moral sense of the people imperfectly supports the law itself. The great body of the people abide by the dry legal obligation in both cases, and a few break over in each. This, I think, cannot be perfectly cured, and it would be worse in both cases after the separation of the sections than before. The foreign slave-trade, now imperfectly suppressed, would be ultimately revived, without restriction, in one section; while fugitive slaves, now only partially surrendered, would not be surrendered at all by the other.

"Physically speaking, we cannot separate; we cannot remove our respective sections from each other, nor build an impassable wall between them. A husband and wife may be divorced, and go out of the presence and beyond the reach of each other, but the different parts of our country cannot do this. They cannot remain face to face; and intercourse, either amicable or hostile, must continue between them. Is it possible, then, to make that intercourse more advantageous or more satisfactory after separation than before? Can aliens make treaties easier than friends can make laws? Can treaties be more faithfully enforced between aliens than laws can among friends? Suppose you go to war, you cannot fight always; and when, after much loss on both sides, and no gain on either, you cease fighting, the identical questions as to terms of intercourse are again upon you.

"This country, with its institutions, belongs to the people who inhabit it. Whenever they shall grow weary of the existing Government, they can exercise their constitutional right of amending, or their revolutionary right to dismember or overthrow it. I cannot be ignorant of the fact that many worthy and patriotic citizens are desirous of having the National Constitution amended. While I make no recommendation of amendment, I fully recognize the full authority of the people over the whole subject, to be exercised in either of the modes prescribed in the instrument itself, and I should, under existing circumstances, favor rather than oppose, a fair opportunity being afforded the people to act upon it.

"I will venture to add, that to me the Convention mode seems preferable, in that it allows amendments to originate with the people themselves, instead of only permitting them to take or reject propositions originated by others not especially chosen for the purpose, and which might not be precisely such as they would wish either to accept or refuse. I understand that a proposed amendment to the Constitution (which amendment, however, I have not seen) has passed Congress, to the effect that the Federal Government shall never interfere with the domestic institutions of States, including that of persons held to service. To avoid misconstruction of what I have said, I depart from my purpose not to speak of particular amendments, so far as to say that, holding such a provision to now be implied constitutional law, I have no objection to its being made express and irrevocable.

"The Chief Magistrate derives all his authority from the people, and they have conferred none upon him to fix the terms for the separation of the States. The people themselves, also, can do this if they choose, but the Executive, as such, has nothing to do with it. His duty is to administer the present Government as it came to his hands, and to transmit it unimpaired by him to his successor. Why should there not be a patient confidence in the ultimate justice of the people? Is there any better or equal hope in the world? In our present differences is either party without faith of being in the right? If the Almighty Ruler of nations, with his eternal truth and justice, be on your side of the North, or on yours of the South, that truth and that justice will surely prevail by the judgment of his great tribunal, the American people. By the frame of the Government under which we live, this same people have wisely given their public servants but little power for mischief, and have with equal wisdom provided for the return of that little to their own hands at very short intervals. While the people retain their virtue and vigilance, no administration, by any extreme wickedness or folly, can very seriously injure the government in the short space of four years.

" My countrymen, one and all, think calmly and well upon

this whole subject. Nothing valuable can be lost by taking time.

"If there be an object to hurry any of you, in hot haste, to a step which you would never take deliberately, that object will be frustrated by taking time: but no good object can be frustrated by it.

"Such of you as are now dissatisfied, still have the old Constitution unimpaired, and on the sensitive point, the laws of your own framing under it; while the new administration will have no immediate power, if it would, to change either.

"If it were admitted that you who are dissatisfied hold the right side in the dispute, there is still no single reason for precipitate action. Intelligence, patriotism, Christianity, and a firm reliance on Him who has never yet forsaken this favored land, are still competent to adjust, in the best way, all our present difficulties.

"In your hands, my dissatisfied fellow-countrymen, and not in mine, is the momentous issue of civil war. The Government will not assail you.

"You can have no conflict without being yourselves the aggressors. You have no oath registered in Heaven to destroy the Government; while I shall have the most solemn one to 'preserve, protect, and defend' it.

"I am loath to close. We are not enemies, but friends. We must not be enemies. Though passion may have strained, it must not break our bonds of affection.

"The mystic cords of memory, stretching from every battlefield and patriot grave to every living heart and hearthstone all over this broad land, will yet swell the chorus of the Union, when again touched, as surely they will be, by the better angels of our nature."

ANNOUNCEMENT OF THE EMANCIPATION PROCLAMATION.

I, ABRAHAM LINCOLN, President of the United States of America, and Commander-in-chief of the Army and Navy thereof, do hereby proclaim and declare, that hereafter, as heretofore, the war will be prosecuted for the object of practically restoring the constitutional relation between the United States and the people thereof, in those States in which that relation is, or may be, suspended or disturbed; that it is my purpose, upon the next meeting of Congress, to again recommend the adoption of a practical measure tendering pecuniary aid to the free acceptance or rejection of all the Slave States, so-called, the people whereof may not then be in rebellion against the United States, and which States may then have voluntarily adopted, or thereafter may voluntarily adopt, the immediate or gradual abolishment of slavery within their respective limits, and that the effort to colonize persons of African descent, with their consent, upon the continent or elsewhere, with the previously obtained consent of the government existing there, will be continued; that on the first day of January, in the year of our Lord one thousand eight hundred and sixty-three, all persons held as slaves within any State, or any designated part of a State, the people whereof shall then be in rebellion against the United States, SHALL BE THEN, THENCEFORWARD AND FOREVER FREE, and the Executive Government of the United States, including the military and naval authority thereof, will recognize and maintain the freedom of such persons, and will do no act or acts to repress such persons, or any of them, in any efforts they may make for their actual freedom; that the Executive will, on the first day of January aforesaid, by proclamation, designate the States and parts of States, if any, in which the people thereof respectively shall be in rebellion against the United States; and the fact that any State, or the people thereof, shall on that day be in good faith represented in the Congress of the United States by members chosen thereto, at elections wherein a majority of the qualified voters of such State shall have participated, shall, in the absence of strong countervailing testimony, be deemed conclusive evidence that such State and the people thereof have not been in rebellion against the United States.

"That attention is hereby called to an Act of Congress, entitled, 'An act to make an additional article of war,' approved March 13, 1862, and which act is in the words and figures following:—

"'*Be it enacted by the Senate and House of Representatives of the United States of America, in Congress assembled*, That hereafter the following shall be promulgated as an additional Article of War for the government of the Army of the United States, and shall be observed and obeyed as such.

"'*Article* —. All officers or persons of the military or naval service of the United States, are prohibited from employing any of the forces under their respective commands for the purpose of returning fugitives from service or labor who may have escaped from any persons to whom such service or labor is claimed to be due; and any officer who shall be found guilty by a court-martial of violating this article, shall be dismissed from the service.

"'*Section* 2. And be it further enacted, That this act shall take effect from and after its passage.'

"Also to the ninth and tenth sections of an act entitled, 'An act to suppress insurrection, to punish treason and rebellion, to seize and confiscate property of rebels, and for other purposes,' approved July 17, 1862, and which sections are in the words and figures following:—

"'*Section* 9. And be it further enacted, That all slaves of persons who shall hereafter be engaged in rebellion against the Government of the United States, or who shall in any way give aid or comfort thereto, escaping from such persons and taking refuge within the lines of the army; and all slaves captured from such persons or deserted by them, and coming under the control of the Government of the United States, and all slaves of such persons found on (or being within) any place occupied by rebel forces, and afterwards occupied by the forces of the United States, shall be deemed captives of war, and shall be forever free of their servitude, and not again held as slaves.

"'*Section* 10. And be it further enacted, That no slave escaping into any State, Territory, or the District of Columbia, from any of the States, shall be delivered up, or in any way impeded or hindered of his liberty, except for crime, or some offence against the laws, unless the person claiming said fugitive shall first make oath that the person to whom the labor or service of such fugitive is alleged to be due, is his lawful owner, and has not been in arms against the United States in the present rebellion, nor in any way given aid and comfort thereto; and no person engaged in the military or naval service of the United States shall, under any pretence whatever, assume to decide on the validity of the claim of any person to the service or labor of any other person, or surrender up any such person to the claimant, on pain of being dismissed from the service.'

"And I do hereby enjoin upon, and order all persons engaged in the military and naval service of the United States to observe, obey, and enforce within their respective spheres of service the act and sections above recited.

"And the executive will in due time recommend that all citizens of the United States, who shall have remained loyal thereto throughout the rebellion, shall (upon the restoration of the constitutional relation between the United States and their respective States and people, if the relation shall have been suspended or disturbed) be compensated for all losses by acts of the United States, including the loss of slaves.

"In witness whereof, I have hereunto set my hand and caused the seal of the United States to be affixed.

"Done at the city of Washington, this twenty-second day of September, in the year of our Lord one thousand eight hundred and sixty-two, and of the Independence of the United States the eighty-seventh.

"By the President: ABRAHAM LINCOLN.

"WILLIAM H. SEWARD, Secretary of State."

PROCLAMATION OF EMANCIPATION.

WHEREAS, On the twenty-second day of September, in the year of our Lord one thousand eight hundred and sixty-two, a proclamation was issued by the President of the United States, containing, among other things, the following, to wit:

That on the first day of January, in the year of our Lord one thousand eight hundred and sixty-three, all persons held as slaves within any State, or any designated part of a State, the people whereof shall then be in rebellion against the United States, shall be thenceforward and forever free, and the Executive Government of the United States, including the military and naval authority thereof, will recognize and maintain the freedom of such persons, and will do no act or acts to repress such persons, or any of them, in any efforts they may make for their actual freedom.

That the Executive will, on the first day of January aforesaid, by proclamation, designate the States and parts of States, if any, in which the people thereof respectively shall then be in rebellion against the United States, and the fact that any State, or the people thereof, shall on that day be in good faith represented in the Congress of the United States by members chosen thereto at elections wherein a majority of the qualified voters of such State shall have participated, shall, in the absence of strong countervailing testimony, be deemed conclusive evidence that such State and the people thereof are not then in rebellion against the United States.

Now, therefore, I, Abraham Lincoln, President of the United States, by virtue of the power in me vested as Commander-in-chief of the Army and Navy of the United States, in time of actual armed rebellion against the authority and Government of the United States, and as a fit and necessary war measure for repressing said rebellion, do, on this first day of January, in the year of our Lord one thousand eight hundred and sixty-three, and in accordance with my purpose so to do, publicly proclaimed for the full period of one hundred days from the day of the first above-mentioned order, designate, as the States and parts of States wherein the people thereof respectively are this day in rebellion against the United States, the following, to wit: Arkansas, Texas, Louisiana, except the parishes of St. Bernard, Plaquemines, Jefferson, St. John, St. Charles, St. James, Ascension, Assumption, Terre Bonne, Lafourche, St. Mary, St. Martin, and Orleans, including the city of New Orleans, Mississippi, Alabama, Florida, Georgia, South Carolina, North Carolina, and Virginia, except the forty-eight counties designated as West Virginia, and also the counties of Berkeley, Accomac, Northampton, Elizabeth City, York, Princess Ann, and Norfolk, including the cities of Norfolk and Portsmouth, and which excepted parts are, for the present, left precisely as if this proclamation were not issued.

And by virtue of the power and for the purpose aforesaid, I do order and declare that all persons held as slaves within said designated States and parts of States are, and henceforward shall be free; and that the Executive Government of the United States, including the military and naval authorities thereof, will recognize and maintain the freedom of said persons.

And I hereby enjoin upon the people so declared to be free, to abstain from all violence, unless in necessary self-defence, and I recommend to them, that in all cases, when allowed, they labor faithfully for reasonable wages.

And I further declare and make known that such persons of suitable condition will be received into the armed service of the United States to garrison forts, positions, stations, and other places, and to man vessels of all sorts in said service.

And upon this, sincerely believed to be an act of justice, warranted by the Constitution, upon military necessity, I invoke the considerate judgment of mankind and the gracious favor of Almighty God.

In witness whereof, I have hereunto set my hand and caused the seal of the United States to be affixed.

Done at the city of Washington, this first day of January, in the year of our Lord one thousand eight hundred and sixty-three, and of the Independence of the United States the eighty-seventh.

By the President: ABRAHAM LINCOLN.

W. H. SEWARD, Secretary of State.

ADDRESS OF THE GENERAL CONFERENCE TO PRESIDENT LINCOLN, WITH THE REPLY OF THE PRESIDENT.

To His Excellency Abraham Lincoln, President of the United States.

The General Conference of the Methodist Episcopal Church, now in session in the city of Philadelphia, representing nearly seven thousand ministers and nearly a million of members, mindful of their duty as Christian citizens, takes the earliest opportunity to express to you the assurance of the loyalty of the Church, her earnest devotion to the interests of the country, and her sympathy with you in the great responsibilities of your high position in this trying hour.

With exultation we point to the record of our church as having never been tarnished by disloyalty. She was the first of the Churches to express, by a deputation of her most distinguished ministers, the promise of support to the Government in the days of Washington. In her Articles of Religion she has enjoined loyalty as a duty, and has ever given to the government her most decided support.

In this present struggle for the nation's life, many thousands of her members, and a large number of her ministers, have rushed to arms to maintain the cause of God and humanity. They have sealed their devotion to their country with their blood on every battle-field of this terrible war.

We regard this dreadful scourge now desolating our land and wasting the nation's life as the result of a most unnatural, utterly unjustifiable rebellion, involving the crime of treason against the best of human governments and sin against God. It required our government to submit to its own dismemberment and destruction, leaving it no alternative but to preserve the national integrity by the use of the national resources. If the government had failed to use its power to preserve the unity of the nation and maintain its authority, it would have been justly exposed to the wrath of heaven, and to the reproach and scorn of the civilized world.

Our earnest and constant prayer is, that this cruel and wicked rebellion may be speedily suppressed; and we pledge you our hearty co-operation in all appropriate means to secure this object.

Loyal and hopeful in national adversity, in prosperity thankful, we most heartily congratulate you on the glorious victories recently gained, and rejoice in the belief that our complete triumph is near.

We believe that our national sorrows and calamities have resulted in a great degree from our forgetfulness of God and oppression of our fellow-men. Chastened by affliction, may the nation humbly repent of her sins, lay aside her haughty pride, honor God in all future legislation, and render justice to all who have been wronged.

We honor you for your proclamations of liberty, and rejoice in all the acts of the government designed to secure freedom to the enslaved.

We trust that when military usages and necessities shall justify interference with established institutions, and the removal of wrongs sanctioned by law, the occasion will be improved, not merely to injure our foes and increase the national resources, but also as an opportunity to recognize our obligations to God and to honor his law. We pray that the time may speedily come when this shall be truly a republican and free country, in no part of which, either state or territory, shall slavery be known.

The prayers of millions of Christians, with an earnestness never manifested for rulers before, daily ascend to heaven that you may be endued with all needed wisdom and power. Actuated by the sentiments of the loftiest and purest patriotism, our prayer shall be continually for the preservation of our country undivided, for the triumph of our cause, and for a permanent peace, gained by the sacrifice of no moral principles, but founded on the word of God, and securing in righteousness liberty and equal rights to all.

Signed in behalf of the General Conference of the Methodist Episcopal Church.

Respectfully submitted,

JOSEPH CUMMINGS, *Chairman.*

PHILADELPHIA, *May* 14, 1864.

PRESIDENT LINCOLN'S REPLY TO THE ADDRESS.

GENTLEMEN: In response to your address allow me to attest the accuracy of its historical statements, indorse the sentiments it expresses, and thank you in the nation's name for the sure promise it gives.

Nobly sustained as the government has been by all the Churches, I would utter nothing which might in the least appear invidious against any. Yet without this it may fairly be said that the Methodist Episcopal Church, not less devoted than the best, is, by its greater numbers, the most important of all. It is no fault in others that the Methodist Church sends more soldiers to the field, more nurses to the hospitals, and more prayers to heaven than any. God bless the Methodist Church! bless all the Churches! and blessed be God! who in this our great trial giveth us the Churches.

[Signed] A. LINCOLN.

SECOND INAUGURAL ADDRESS OF ABRAHAM LINCOLN.

FELLOW-COUNTRYMEN: At this second appearing to take the oath of the Presidential office, there is less occasion for an extended address than there was at the first. Then a statement somewhat in detail of a course to be pursued seemed very fitting and proper. Now, at the expiration of four years, during which public declarations have constantly been called forth on every point and phase of the great contest which still absorbs the attention, and engrosses the energies of the nation, little that is new could be presented.

The progress of our arms, upon which all else chiefly depends, is as well known to the public as to myself, and it is, I trust, reasonably satisfactory and encouraging to all. With high hope for the future, no prediction in regard to it is ventured. On the occasion corresponding to this four years ago, all thoughts were anxiously directed to an impending civil war. All dreaded it, all sought to avoid it. While the inaugural address was being delivered from this place, devoted altogether to saving the Union without war, insurgent agents were in the city seeking to destroy it without war; seeking to dissolve the Union and divide the effects by negotiation.

Both parties deprecated war, but one of them would make war rather than let the nation survive, and the other would accept war rather than let it perish, and the war came.

One-eighth of the whole population were colored slaves, not distributed generally over the Union, but located in the southern part of it. These slaves constituted a peculiar and powerful interest. All knew that this interest was somehow the cause of the war. To strengthen, perpetuate and extend this interest was the object for which the insurgents would rend the Union by war, while the Government claimed no right to do more than to restrict the territorial enlargement of it. Neither party expected the magnitude or the duration which it has already attained. Neither anticipated that the cause of the conflict might cease, even before the conflict itself should cease. Each looked for an easier triumph and a result less fundamental and astounding. Both read the same Bible, and pray to the same God, and each invokes his aid against the other. It may seem strange that any man should dare to ask a just God's assistance in wringing his bread from the sweat of other men's faces. But let us "judge not, that we be not judged."

The prayer of both should not be answered. That of neither has been answered fully. The Almighty has his own purposes. "Woe unto the world because of offences, for it must needs be that offences come, but woe to that man by whom the offence cometh." If we shall suppose that American slavery is one of these offences, which, in the providence of God, must needs come, but which, having continued through his appointed time, he now wills to remove, and that he gives to both North and South this terrible war as the woe due to those by whom the offence came, shall we discern therein any departure from those Divine attributes which the believers in a living God always ascribe to him?

Fondly do we hope, fervently do we pray that this mighty scourge of war may speedily pass away. Yet, if God wills that it continue until all the wealth piled by the bondman's two hundred and fifty years of unrequited toil shall be sunk, and until every drop of blood drawn by the lash shall be paid by another drawn with the sword, as was said three thousand years ago, so still it must be said, that the judgments of the Lord are true and righteous altogether.

With malice towards none, with charity for all, with firmness in the right, as God gives us to see the right, let us strive on to finish the work we are in, to bind up the nation's wound, to care for him who shall have borne the battle, and for his widow and his orphans, to do all which may achieve and cherish a just and lasting peace among ourselves and with all nations.

FUNERAL SERVICES OF MR. LINCOLN AT THE WHITE HOUSE, THE CAPITOL OF THE NATION.

Mr. LINCOLN was assassinated on the night of the 14th of April, 1865.

At 12 o'clock, noon, April, 19th, 1865, the room was filled with weeping friends, the President and Cabinet having entered last.

Rev. Dr. GURLEY, of the Presbyterian Church, whose church Mr. Lincoln and family generally attended in Washington, announced the order of exercises.

Rev. Dr. HALL read, very impressively, the funeral services of the Episcopal Church, commencing "I am the resurrection and the life, &c."

This solemn service was followed by a fervent extemporaneous prayer, by Rev. Bishop Simpson, of the Methodist Episcopal Church.

THE BISHOP'S PRAYER.

ALMIGHTY GOD, our Heavenly Father, as with smitten and suffering hearts we come into Thy presence, we pray, in the name of our blessed Redeemer, that Thou wouldst pour upon us Thy Holy Spirit, that all our thoughts and acts may be acceptable in Thy sight. We adore Thee for all Thy glorious perfections. We praise Thee for the revelation which Thou hast given us in Thy works and in Thy Word. By thee all worlds exist. All beings live through Thee. Thou raisest up kingdoms and empires, and castest them down. By Thee kings reign, and princes decree righteousness. In Thy hand are the issues of life and death. We confess before Thee the magnitude of our sins and transgressions, both as individuals and as a nation. We implore Thy mercy for the sake of our Redeemer. Forgive us all our iniquities. If it please Thee, remove Thy chastening hand from us, and, though we be unworthy, turn away from us Thine anger, and let the light of Thy countenance again shine upon us.

At this solemn hour, as we mourn for the death of our President, who was stricken down by the hand of an assassin, grant us also the grace to bow in submission to Thy holy will. May we recognize thy hand high above all human agencies, and thy power as controlling all events, so that "the wrath of man shall praise Thee, and that the remainder of wrath thou wilt restrain." Humbled under the suffering we have endured and the great afflictions through which we have passed, may we not be called upon to offer other sacrifices. May the lives of all our officers, both civil and military, be guarded by Thee; and let no violent hand fall upon any of them. Mourning, as we do, for the mighty dead by whose remains we stand, we would yet lift our hearts unto Thee in grateful acknowledgment for Thy kindness in giving us so great and noble a President. Thou art glorified in good men, and we praise Thee that Thou didst give him unto us so pure, so honest, so sincere, and so transparent in character. We praise Thee for that kind, affectionate heart, which always swelled with feelings of enlarged benevolence. We bless Thee for what Thou didst enable him to do; that Thou didst give him wisdom to select for his advisers and for his officers, military and naval, those men through whom our country has been carried triumphantly through an unprecedented conflict.

We bless Thee for the success which has attended all their efforts, and for the victories which have crowned our armies; and that Thou didst spare Thy servant until he could behold the dawning of that glorious morning of peace and prosperity which is about to shine upon our land; that he was enabled to go up as Thy servant of old upon Mount Pisgah, and catch a glimpse of the promised land. Though his lips are silent and his arm is powerless, we thank Thee that Thou didst strengthen him, to speak words that cheer the hearts of the suffering and the oppressed; and to write that declaration of emancipation which has given him an immortal record; that though the hand of the assassin has struck him to the ground, it could not destroy the work which he has done, nor forge again the chains which he has broken. And while we mourn that he has passed away, we are grateful that his work was so fully accomplished, and that the acts which he has performed will forever remain.

We implore Thy blessing upon his bereaved family. Thou husband of the widow, bless her who, broken-hearted and sorrowing, feels oppressed with unutterable anguish. Cheer the loneliness of the pathway which lies before her, and grant to her such consolations of Thy Spirit, and such hopes through the resurrection, that she shall feel that "Earth hath no sorrows which Heaven cannot heal."

Let Thy blessings rest upon his sons; pour upon them the spirit of wisdom. Be Thou the guide of their youth; prepare them for usefulness in society, for happiness in all their relations. May the remembrance of their father's counsels and their father's noble acts ever stimulate them to glorious deeds, and at last may they be heirs of everlasting life.

Command Thy richest benedictions to descend upon the successor of our lamented President. Grant unto him wisdom, energy, and firmness for the responsible duties to which he has been called. May he not only be a praise to them that do well, but may he so be a terror to evil doers as not to bear the sword in vain. May he, his cabinet, officers and generals who shall lead his armies, and the brave soldiers in the field, be so guided by Thy counsels that they shall speedily complete the great work which he had so successfully carried forward.

Let Thy blessing rest upon our country. Grant unto us all a fixed and strong determination never to cease our efforts until our glorious Union shall be fully re-established.

Around the remains of our loved President may we covenant together by every possible means to give ourselves to our country's service until every vestige of this rebellion shall have been wiped out, and until slavery, its cause, shall be forever eradicated, and freedom shall reign from the Lakes to the Gulf, and from the Atlantic to the Pacific.

Preserve us, we pray Thee, from all complications with foreign nations. Give us hearts to act justly toward all nations, and grant unto them hearts to act justly toward us, that universal peace and happiness may fill our earth. We rejoice that in this afflicting dispensation Thou hast given an additional evidence of the strength of our nation. We bless Thee that no tumult has arisen, that there has been no conflict for power, and that in peace and harmony our Government moves onward; and that Thou hast shown, through us, to all nations that Republics possess every element of strength, and that, in the midst of this terrible trial, our Government is the strongest on the face of the earth.

In this solemn presence may we feel that we too are mortal. May the sense of our responsibility to God rest upon us; may we repent of every sin; and may we consecrate anew unto Thee all the time, and all the talents which Thou hast given us; and may we so fulfil our allotted duties that finally we may have communion with the good and wise and great, who now surround Thy glorious throne! Hear us while we unite in praying with Thy Church in all lands, and in all ages, even as Thou hast taught us, saying—

Our Father which art in heaven, Hallowed be Thy name. Thy kingdom come. Thy will be done in earth as it is in heaven. Give us this day our daily bread. And forgive us our debts, as we forgive our debtors. And lead us not into temptation, but deliver us from evil. For thine is the kingdom, and the power, and the glory, for ever. Amen.

FUNERAL ORATION, BY REV. DR. GURLEY, OF THE PRESBYTERIAN CHURCH.

As we stand here to-day mourners around this coffin, and around the lifeless remains of our beloved Chief Magistrate, we recognize and we adore the sovereignty of God. His throne is in the heavens, and his kingdom ruleth over all. He hath done and hath permitted to be done whatsoever He pleased. Clouds and darkness are round about Him; righteousness and judgment are the habitation of His throne. His way is in the sea and His path in the great waters, and His footsteps are not known. Canst thou by searching find out God? Canst thou find out the Almighty unto perfection? It is as high as heaven. What canst thou do? Deeper than hell. What canst thou know? The measure thereof is longer than the earth and broader than the sea. If He cut off and shut up, or gather together; then who can hinder Him? For He knoweth vain men; He seeth wickedness. Also, will He not then consider it? We bow before His infinite majesty. We bow—we weep—we worship.

> "There reason fails with all her powers,
> There faith prevails, and love adores."

It was a cruel, cruel hand, that dark hand of the assassin, which smote our honored, wise, and noble President, and filled the land with sorrow. But above and beyond that hand there is another, which we must see and acknowledge. It is the chastening hand of a wise and faithful Father. He gives us the bitter cup; and the cup that our Father hath given us, shall we not drink it? God of the just, Thou gavest us the cup. We yield to Thy behest, and drink it up. Whom the Lord loveth He chasteneth. Oh, how these blessed words have cheered and strengthened and sustained us through all these long and weary years of civil strife, while our friends and brothers on so many ensanguined fields were falling and dying for the cause of liberty and Union. Let them cheer and strengthen and sustain us to-day. True, this new sorrow and chastening has come in such an hour and in such a way as we thought not, and it bears the impress of a rod that is very heavy, and of a mystery that is very deep. That such a life should be sacrificed at such a time, by such a foul and diabolical agency; that the man at the head of the nation, whom the people had learned to trust with a confiding and a loving confidence, and upon whom more than upon any other were centred, under God, our best hopes for the true and speedy pacification of the country, the restoration of the Union, and the return of harmony and love; that he should be taken from us, and taken just as the prospect of peace was brightly opening upon our torn and bleeding country, and just as he was beginning to be animated and gladdened with the hope of ere long enjoying with the people the blessed fruit and reward of his and their toil and care and patience, and self-sacrificing devotion to the interests of liberty and the Union—oh! it is a mysterious and a most afflicting dispensation. But it is our Father in heaven, the God of our fathers, who permits us to be so suddenly and sorely smitten, and we know that His judgments are right, and that in faithfulness He has afflicted us in the midst of our rejoicings. We needed this stroke, this dealing, this discipline, and therefore He has sent it. Let us remember our affliction has not come forth of the dust, and our trouble has not sprung out of the ground. Through and beyond all second causes let us look and see the sovereign permissive agency of the first great cause. It is His prerogative to bring light out of darkness and good out of evil. Surely the wrath of man shall praise Him, and the remainder of wrath He will restrain. In the light of a clear day we may yet see that the wrath which planned and perpetrated the death of the President was overruled by

Him, whose judgments are unsearchable and His ways past finding out, for the highest welfare of all those interests which are so dear to the Christian, patriot, and philanthropist, and for which a loyal people have made such an unexampled sacrifice of treasure and of blood. Let us not be faithless, but believing.

> "Blind unbelief is sure to err,
> And scan his work in vain;
> God is his own interpreter,
> And he will make it plain."

We will wait for His interpretation, and we will wait in faith, nothing doubting. He who has led us so well, and defended and prospered us so wonderfully during the last four years of toil, and struggle, and sorrow, will not forsake us now. He may chasten, but He will not destroy. He may purify us more and more in the furnace of trial, but He will not consume us: no, no. He has chosen us, as He did His people of old in the furnace of affliction, and He has said of us, as He said of them, "This people have I formed for myself; they shall show forth my praise." Let our principal anxiety now be that this new sorrow may be a sanctified sorrow; that it may lead us to deeper repentance, to a more humbling sense of our dependence upon God, and to the more unreserved consecration of ourselves and all that we have to the cause of truth and justice, of law and order, of liberty and good government, of pure and undefiled religion. Then, though "weeping may endure for a night, joy will come in the morning." Blessed be God, despite of the great, and sudden, and temporary darkness, the morning has begun to dawn—the morning of a bright and glorious day, such as our country has never seen. That day will come and not tarry, and the death of a hundred presidents and their cabinets can never, never prevent it. While we are hopeful, however, let us also be humble. The occasion calls us to prayerful and tearful humiliation. It demands of us that we lie low, very low, before Him who has stricken us for our sins. Oh, that all our rulers and all our people may bow in the dust to-day beneath the chastening hand of God, and may their voices go up to Him as one voice, and their hearts go up to Him as one heart, pleading with Him for mercy, and for grace to sanctify our great and sore bereavement, and for wisdom to guide us in this our time of need. Such a united cry and pleading will not be in vain. It will enter into the ear and heart of Him who sits upon the throne, and He will say to us as to his ancient Israel, "In a little wrath I hid my face from thee for a moment; but with everlasting kindness will I have mercy upon thee, saith the Lord, thy Redeemer." I have said that the people confided in the late lamented President with a full and a loving confidence. Probably no man since the days of Washington was ever so deeply and firmly imbedded and enshrined in the very hearts of the people as Abraham Lincoln. Nor was it a mistaken confidence and love. He deserved it—deserved it well—deserved it all. He merited it by his character, by his acts, and by the whole tenor and tone and spirit of his life. He was simple and sincere, plain and honest, trustful and just, benevolent and kind. His perceptions were quick and clear, his judgments were calm and accurate, and his purposes were good and pure, beyond a question. Always and everywhere he aimed and endeavored to be right and to do right. His integrity was thorough, all pervading, all controlling, and incorruptible. It was the same in every place and relation. In the consideration and the control of matters, great or small, the same firm and steady principle of power and beauty, that shed a clear and crowning lustre upon all his other excellences of mind and heart and recommended him to his fellow-citizens as the man who, in a time of unexampled peril, when the very life of the nation was at stake, should be chosen to occupy—in the country and for the country—its highest post of power and responsibility. How wisely and well, how purely and faithfully, how firmly and steadily, how justly and successfully, he did occupy that post and meet its grave demands, in circumstances of surprising trial and difficulty, is known to you all, is known to the country and the world. He comprehended from the first the perils to which treason had exposed the freest and best government on the earth, the vast interests of liberty and humanity that were to be saved or lost forever, in the urgent impending conflict. He rose to the dignity and momentousness of the occasion, saw his duty as Chief Magistrate of a great and imperilled people, and he determined to do his duty and his whole duty, seeking the guidance and leaning upon the arm of Him of whom it is written, "He giveth power to the faint, and to them that have no might He increases their strength." Yes, he leaned upon His arm; he recognized and received the truth that 'the kingdom is the Lord's, and He is the Governor among the nations.' He remembered that 'God is in history,' and he felt that nowhere had His hand and His mercy been so marvellously conspicuous as in the history of this nation. He hoped and prayed that 'that same hand would continue to guide us, and that same mercy continue to abound to us in the time of our greatest need.' I speak what I know, and testify what I have often heard him say, when I affirm that that guidance and mercy were the prop on which he humbly and habitually leaned; that they were the best hope he had for himself and for his country. Hence when he was leaving his home in Illinois and coming to this city to take his seat in the executive chair of a disturbed and troubled nation; he said to the old and tried friends who gathered joyfully around him and bade him farewell, 'I leave you with this request—pray for me.' They did pray for him. And millions of others prayed for him. Nor did they pray in vain. Their prayers were heard, and the answer appears in all his subsequent history. It shines forth with a heavenly radiance in the whole course and tenor of his administration, from its commencement to its close. God raised him up for a great and glorious mission, furnished him for his work, and aided him in its accomplishment. Nor was it merely by strength of mind and honesty of heart and purity and pertinacity of purpose that he furnished him in addition to these things; he gave him a calm and abiding confidence in the overruling providence of God, and in the ultimate triumph of truth and righteousness through the power and blessing of God. This confidence strengthened him in all his hours of anxiety and toil, and inspired him with calm and cheering hope, when others were inclining to despondency and gloom. Never shall I forget the emphasis and the deep emotion with which he said in this very room to a company of clergymen and others, who called to pay him their respects in the darkest days of our civil conflict: "Gentlemen, my hope of success in this great and terrible struggle rests on that immutable foundation, the justice and goodness of God." And when events are very threatening, and prospects very dark, "I still hope that in some way which man cannot see, all will be well in the end; because our cause is just and God is on our side." Such was his sublime and holy faith, and it was an anchor to his soul, both sure and steadfast; it made him firm and strong; and emboldened him in the pathway of duty, however rugged and perilous it might be. It made him valiant for the right, for the cause of God and humanity, and it held him in steady, patient, and unswerving adherence to a policy of administration which, he thought, and which we all now think, both God and humanity required him to adopt. We admired and loved him on many accounts, for strong and various reasons. We admired his childlike simplicity, freedom from guile and deceit; his stanch and sterling integrity; his kind and forgiving temper; his industry and patience; his persistent, self-sacrificing devotion to all the duties of his eminent position, from the least to the greatest; his readiness to hear and consider the cause of the poor and humble, the suffering and the oppressed; his charity towards those who questioned the correctness of his opinions and the wisdom of his policy; his wonderful skill in reconciliating the differences among the friends of the Union, leading them away from obstructions, and inducing them to work together and harmoniously for the common weal; his true and enlarged philanthropy that knew no distinction of color or race, but regarded all men as brethren, and endowed alike by their Creator with certain inalienable rights, amongst which are life, liberty, and the pursuit of happiness; his inflexible purpose that what freedom had gained in our terrible strife should never be lost, and that the end of the war should be the end of slavery, and as a consequence of rebellion; his readiness to spend and be spent for the attainment of such a triumph— a triumph the blessed fruits of which should be as widespreading as the earth and as enduring as the sun. All these things commanded and fixed our admiration and the admiration of the world, and stamped upon his character and life the unmistakable impress of greatness. But, more sublime than any or all of these, more holy and influential, more beautiful and strong and sustaining was his abiding confidence in God, and in the final triumph of truth and righteousness, through Him and for His sake. This was his noblest virtue, his grandest principle, the secret alike of his strength, his patience, and his success; and this, it seems to me, after being near him steadily and with him often for more than four years, is the principle by which more than by any other, he being dead, yet speaketh.

Yes, by his steady enduring confidence in God, and in the complete ultimate success of the cause of God, which is the cause of humanity, more than in any other way does he now speak to us, and to the nation he loved and served so well. By this he speaks to his successor in office, and charges him to have faith in God. By this he speaks to the members of his Cabinet, the men with whom he counselled so often and was associated with so long, and he charges them to have faith in God. By this he speaks to all who occupy positions of influence and authority in these sad and troublesome times, and he charges them all to have faith in God. By this he speaks to this great people as they sit in sackcloth to-day and weep for him with a bitter wailing, and refuse to be comforted; and he charges them to have faith in God; and by this he will speak through the ages, and to all rulers and peoples in every land, and his message to them will be: "Cling to liberty and right; battle for them; bleed for them; die for them, if need be, and have confidence in God." Oh! that the voice of this testimony may sink down into our hearts to-day and every day, and into the heart of the nation, and exert its appropriate influence upon our feelings, our faith, our patience and our devotion to the cause, now dearer to us than ever before, because consecrated by the blood of the most conspicuous defender, its wisest and most fondly trusted friend. He is dead, but the God in whom he trusted lives, and he can guide and strengthen his successor as he guided and strengthened him. He is dead, but the memory of his virtues, of his wise and patriotic counsels and labors, of his calm and steady faith in God lives, is precious, and will be a power for good in the country quite down to the end of time. He is dead; but the cause he so ardently loved, so ably, patiently, faithfully represented and defended, not for himself only, not for us only, but for all people, in all their coming generations, till time shall be no more—that cause survives his fall, and will survive it. The light of its brightening prospects flashes cheeringly to-day around the gloom occasioned by his duties, and the language of God's united providences is telling us that, though the friends of liberty die, liberty itself is immortal; there is no assassin strong enough, and no weapon deadly enough to quench its inextinguishable life or arrest its onward march to the conquest and empire of the world. This is our confidence and this is our consolation as we weep and mourn to-day. Though our beloved President is slain, our beloved country is saved, and so we sing of mercy as well as of judgment. Tears of gratitude mingle with those of sorrow, while there is also the dawning of a brighter, happier day, upon our stricken and weary land. God be praised that our fallen chief lived long enough to see the day dawn and the day star of joy and peace arise upon the nation. He saw it and he was glad. Alas! alas! he only saw the dawn. When the sun has risen full orbed, and a glorious and a happy reunited people are rejoicing in its light, it will shine upon his grave. But that grave will be a precious and a consecrated spot. The friends of liberty and of the Union will repair to it in years and ages to come to pronounce the memory of its occupant blessed, and gathering from his very ashes and from the rehearsal of his deeds and virtues fresh incentives to patriotism. They will then renew their vows of fidelity to their country and their God. And now I know not that I can more appropriately conclude this discourse, which is but a sincere and simple utterance of the heart, than by addressing to our departed President, with some slight modification, the language which Tacitus, in his life of Agricola, addressed to his venerated and departed father-in-law: "With you we may now congratulate. You are blessed, not only because your life was a career of glory, but because you were released when, your country safe, it was happiness to die. We have lost a parent, and, in our distress, it is now an addition to our heartfelt sorrows that we had it not in our power to commune with you on the bed of languishing and receive your last embrace. Your dying words would have been ever dear to us. Your commands we should have treasured up and graved them on our hearts. This sad comfort we have lost, and the wound for that reason pierces deeper. From the world of spirits behold your disconsolate family and people. Exalt our minds from fond regret and unavailing grief to the contemplation of your virtues. These we must not lament. It were impiety to sully them with a tear. To cherish their memory, to embalm them with our praises, and so far as we can to emulate your bright example, will be the truest mark of your respect, the best tribute we can offer. Your wife will thus preserve the memory of the best of husbands, and thus your children will prove their final piety. By dwelling constantly on your words and actions they will have an illustrious character before their eyes; and not content with the base image of your mortal frame; they will have what is more valuable—the form and features of your mind. Busts and statues, like their originals, are frail and perishable. The soul is formed of finer elements, and its inward form is not to be expressed by the hand of an artist with unconscious matter. Our manners and our morals may in some degree trace the resemblance. All of you that gained our love and raised our admiration still subsist, and will ever subsist, preserved in the minds of men, the register of ages and the records of fame. Others, matured on the stages of life, and who were the worthies of a former day, will sink for want of a faithful historian into the common lot of oblivion, inglorious and unremembered; but you, our lamented friend and head, delineated with truth and fairly consigned to posterity, will survive yourself and triumph over the injuries of time."

FUNERAL ORATION OF BISHOP SIMPSON AT SPRINGFIELD, ILLINOIS.

Rev. BISHOP SIMPSON, of the Methodist Episcopal Church, was a great favorite with the late President of the United States. In the summer of 1864, at the United States Sanitary Fair held in Philadelphia, the President was expected to deliver the opening address, but public duties and executive labors prevented him from being able to meet the expectations of the people. This was a great disappointment. The President atoned for this by enlisting the services of his eloquent and reverend friend, Bishop Simpson. As thousands of living witnesses who heard that thrilling and patriotic speech can testify, the President did not make a mistake in delegating to that Methodist Bishop this responsible task.

Bishop Simpson was again selected by the representatives of his illustrious but departed friend, to deliver the funeral oration at Springfield, Illinois, his former home, and his resting-place, until "this corruptible shall put on incorruption, and this mortal shall put on immortality."

FELLOW-CITIZENS OF ILLINOIS, AND OF MANY PARTS OF OUR ENTIRE UNION: Near the capital of this large and growing State of Illinois, in the midst of this beautiful grove, and at the open mouth of the vault which has just received the remains of our fallen chieftain, we gather to pay a tribute of respect and drop the tears of sorrow around the ashes of the mighty dead. A little more than four years ago, he left his plain and quiet home in yonder city, receiving the parting words of the concourse of friends who, in the midst of the dropping of the gentle shower, gathered around him. He spoke of the pain of parting from the place where he had lived for a quarter of a century, where his children had been born, and his home had been rendered so pleasant by friendly associations. And as he left he made an earnest request in the hearing of some who are present at this hour, that, as he was about to enter upon responsibilities which he believed to be greater than any which had fallen upon any man since the days of Washington, the people would offer up prayers that God would aid and sustain him in the work which they had given him to do.

His company left your quiet city. But as it went, snares were in waiting for the chief magistrate. Scarcely did he escape the dangers of the way or the hands of the assassin as he neared Washington, and I believe he escaped only through the vigilance of the officers and the prayers of the people; so that the blow was suspended for more than four years, which was at last permitted, through the providence of God, to fall.

How different the occasion which witnessed his departure from that which witnessed his return! Doubtless you expected to take him by the hand, to feel the warm grasp which you had felt in other days and to see the tall form walking among you which you had delighted to honor in years past. But he was never permitted to return until he came with lips mute and silent, his frame encoffined, and a weeping nation following as his mourners. Such a scene as his return to you was never witnessed. Among the events of history there have been great processions of mourners. There was one for the patriarch Jacob, which went up from Egypt, and the Egyptians wondered at the evidences of reverence and filial affection which came from the hearts of the Israelites. There was mourning when Moses fell upon the heights of Pisgah and was hid from human view. There have been mournings in the kingdoms of the earth when kings and warriors have fallen. But never was there in the history of man such mourning as that which has accompanied this funeral procession, and has gathered around the mortal remains of him who was our loved one, and who now sleeps among us. If we glance at the procession which followed him, we see how the nation stood aghast. Tears filled the eyes of manly, sunburnt faces. Strong men, as they clasped the hands of their friends, were not able in words to find vent for their grief. Women and little children caught up the tidings as they ran through the land, and were melted into tears. The nation stood still. Men left their ploughs in the fields, and asked what the end should be. The hum of manufactories ceased, and the sound of the hammer was not heard. Busy merchants closed their doors; and in the exchange gold passed no more from hand to hand. Though three weeks have elapsed, the nation has scarcely breathed easily yet. A mournful silence is abroad upon the land; nor is this mourning confined to any class or to any district of country. Men of all political parties, and of all religious creeds, have united in paying this mournful tribute. The archbishop of the Roman Catholic Church in New York and a Protestant minister walked side by side in the sad procession, and a Jewish rabbi performed a part of the solemn services.

Here are gathered around his tomb the representatives of the army and navy, senators, judges, governors, and officers of all the branches of the government. Here, too, are members of civic processions, with men and women from the humblest as well as the highest occupations. Here, and there, too, are tears, as sincere and warm as any that drop, which come from the eyes of those whose kindred and whose race have been freed from their chains by him whom they mourn as their deliverer. More persons have gazed on the face of the departed than ever looked upon the face of any other departed man. More have looked on the procession for 1600 miles or more—by night and by day—by sunlight, dawn, twilight, and by torchlight, than ever before watched the progress of a procession.

We ask why this wonderful mourning—this great procession? I answer, first, a part of the interest has arisen from the times in which we live, and in which he that had fallen was a principal actor. It is a principle of our nature that feelings, once excited, turn readily from the object by which they are excited to some other object which may for the time being take possession of the mind. Another principle is, the deepest affections of our hearts gather around some human form in which are incarnated the living thoughts and ideas of the passing age. If we look then at the times, we see an age of excitement. For four years the popular heart has been stirred to its inmost depth. War had come upon us, dividing families, separating nearest and dearest friends—a war, the extent and magnitude of which no one could estimate—a war in which the blood of brethren was shed by a brother's hand. A call for soldiers was made by this voice now hushed, and all over the land, from hill to mountain, from plain to valley, there sprang up thousands of bold hearts, ready to go forth and save our national Union. This feeling of excitement was transformed next into a feeling of deep grief because of the dangers in which our country was placed. Many said: "Is it possible to save our nation?" Some in our country, and nearly all the leading men in other countries, declared it to be impossible to maintain the Union; and many an honest and patriotic heart was deeply pained with apprehensions of common ruin; and many, in grief, and almost in despair, anxiously inquired: What shall the end of these things be? In addition to this, wives had given their husbands, mothers their sons, the pride and joy of their hearts. They saw them put on the uniform, they saw them take the martial step, and they tried to hide their deep feeling of sadness. Many dear ones slept upon the battle-field never to return again, and there was mourning in every mansion and in every cabin in our broad land. Then came a feeling of deeper sadness as the story came of prisoners tortured to death or starved through the mandates of those who are called the representatives of chivalry, and who claimed to be the honorable ones of the earth; and as we read the stories of frames attenuated and reduced to mere skeletons, our grief turned partly into horror and partly into a cry for vengeance.

Then this feeling was changed to one of joy. There came signs of the end of this rebellion. We followed the career of our glorious generals. We saw our army, under the command of the brave officer who is guiding this procession, climb up the heights of Lookout Mountain, and drive the rebels from their strongholds. Another brave general swept through Georgia, South and North Carolina, and drove the combined armies of the rebels before him, while the honored lieutenant-general held Lee and his hosts in a death grasp.

Then the tidings came that Richmond was evacuated, and that Lee had surrendered. The bells rang merrily all over the land. The booming of cannon was heard; illuminations and torch-light processions manifested the general joy, and families were looking for the speedy return of their loved ones from the field of battle. Just in the midst of this wildest joy, in one hour—nay, in one moment—the tidings thrilled throughout the land that Abraham Lincoln, the best of presidents, had perished by the hands of an assassin; and then all the feelings which had been gathering for four years, in forms of excitement, grief, horror, and joy, turned into one wail of woe—a sadness inexpressible—an anguish unutterable. But it is not the times merely which caused this mourning. The mode of his death must be taken into the account. Had he died on a bed of illness, with kind friends around him; had the sweat of death been wiped from his brow by gentle hands, while he was yet conscious; could he have had power to speak words of affection to his stricken widow, or words of counsel to us like those which we heard in his parting inaugural at Washington, which shall now be immortal—how it would have softened or assuaged something of the grief. There might, at least, have been preparation for the event. But no moment of warning was given to him or to us. He was stricken down, too, when his hopes for the end of the rebellion were bright, and prospects of a joyous life were before him. There was a cabinet meeting that day, said to have been the most cheerful and happy of any held since the beginning of the rebellion. After this meeting he talked with his friends, and spoke of the four years of tempest, of the storm being over, and of the four years of pleasure and joy now awaiting him, as the weight of care and anxiety would be taken from his mind, and he could have happy days with his family again. In the midst of these anticipations he left his house never to return alive. The evening was Good Friday, the saddest day in the whole calendar for the Christian Church—henceforth in this country to be made sadder, if possible, by the memory of our nation's loss; and so filled with grief was every Christian heart, that even all the joyous thought of Easter Sunday failed to remove the crushing sorrow under which the true worshipper bowed in the house of God.

But the great cause of this mourning is to be found in the man himself. Mr. Lincoln was no ordinary man. I believe the conviction has been growing on the nation's mind, as it certainly has been on my own, especially in the last years of his administration, that, by the hand of God, he was especially singled out to guide our government in these troublesome times, and it seems to me that the hand of God may be traced in many of the events connected with his history. First, then, I recognize this in the physical education which he received, and which prepared him for enduring herculean labors. In the toils of his boyhood and the labors of his manhood, God was giving him an iron frame. Next to this was his identification with the heart of the great people, understanding their feelings because he was one of them, and connected with them in their movements and life. His education was simple. A few months spent in the school-house gave him the elements of education. He read few books, but mastered all he read. *Pilgrim's Progress*, *Æsop's Fables*, and the *Life of Washington*, were his favorites. In these we recognize the works which gave the bias to his character, and which partly moulded his style. His early life, with its varied struggles, joined him indissolubly to the working masses, and no elevation in society diminished his respect for the sons of toil. He knew what it was to fell the tall trees of the forest, and to stem the current of the broad Mississippi. His home was in the growing West, the heart of the republic, and, invigorated by the winds which swept over its prairies, he learned lessons of self-reliance which sustained him in seasons of adversity.

His genius was soon recognized, as true genius always will be, and he was placed in the legislature of his State. Already acquainted with the principles of law, he devoted his thoughts to matters of public interest, and began to be looked on as the coming statesman. As early as 1839 he presented resolutions in the legislature asking for emancipation in the District of Columbia, when, with but rare exceptions, the whole popular mind of his State was opposed to the measure. From that hour he was a steady and uniform friend of humanity, and was preparing for the conflict of later years.

If you ask me on what mental characteristic his greatness rested, I answer, on a quick and ready perception of facts; on a memory usually tenacious and retentive; and on a logical turn of mind, which followed sternly and unwaveringly every link in the chain of thought on every subject which he was called to investigate. I think there have been minds more broad in their character, more comprehensive in their scope, but I doubt if there ever has been a man who could follow step by step, with more logical power, the points which he desired to illustrate. He gained this power by the close study of geometry, and by a determination to perceive the truth in all its relations and simplicity, and, when found, to utter it.

It is said of him that in childhood when he had any difficulty, in listening to a conversation, to ascertain what people meant, if he retired to rest he could not sleep till he tried to understand the precise points intended, and when understood, to frame language to convey it in a clearer manner to others. Who that has read his messages fails to perceive the directness and simplicity of his style? And this very trait, which was scoffed at and decried by opponents, is now recognized as one of the strong points of that mighty mind which has so powerfully influenced the destiny of this nation, and which shall, for ages to come, influence the destiny of humanity.

It was not, however, chiefly by his mental faculties that he gained such control over mankind. His moral power gave him preëminence. The convictions of men, that Abraham Lincoln was an honest man, led them to yield to his guidance. As has been said of Cobden, whom he greatly resembled, he made all men feel a sense of himself—a recognition of individuality—a self-relying power. They saw in him a man who they believed would do what is right, regardless of all consequences. It was this moral feeling which gave him the greatest hold on the people, and made his utterances almost oracular. When the nation was angered by the perfidy of foreign nations in allowing privateers to be fitted out, he uttered the significant expression, "One war at a time," and it stilled the national heart. When his own friends were divided as to what steps should be taken as to slavery, that simple utterance, "I will save the Union, if I can, with slavery; if not, slavery must perish, for the Union must be preserved," became the rallying word. Men felt the struggle was for the Union, and all other questions must be subsidiary.

But, after all, by the acts of a man shall his fame be perpetuated. What are his acts? Much praise is due to the men who aided him. He called able counsellors around him—some of whom have displayed the highest order of talent united with the purest and most devoted patriotism. He summoned able generals into the field—men who have borne the sword as bravely as ever any human arm has borne it. He had the aid of prayerful and thoughtful men everywhere. But, under his own guiding hands, wise counsels were combined and great movements conducted.

Turn towards the different departments. We had an unorganized militia, a mere skeleton army; yet, under his care, that army has been enlarged into a force which, for skill, intelligence, efficiency, and bravery, surpasses any which the world has ever seen. Before its veterans the fame of even the renowned veterans of Napoleon shall pale, and the mothers and sisters on these hillsides, and all over the land, shall take to their arms again braver sons and brothers than ever fought in European wars. The reason is obvious. Money, or a desire for fame, collected those armies, or they were rallied to sustain favorite thrones or dynasties; but the armies he called into being fought for liberty, for the Union, and for the right of self-government; and many of them felt that the battles they won were for humanity everywhere and for all time; for I believe that God has not suffered this terrible rebellion to come upon our land merely for a chastisement to us, or as a lesson to our age. There are moments which involve in themselves eternities. There are instants which seem to contain germs which shall develop and bloom forever. Such a moment came in the tide of time to our land, when a question must be settled which affected all the earth. The contest was for human freedom, not for this republic merely; not for the Union simply, but to decide whether the people, as a people, in their entire majesty, were destined to be the government, or whether they were to be subject to tyrants or aristocrats, or to class-rule of any kind. This is the great question for which we have been fighting, and its decision is at hand, and the result of the contest will affect the ages to come. If successful, republics will spread, in spite of monarchs, all over the earth.

I turn from the army to the navy. What was it when

the war commenced? Now we have our ships of war at home and abroad, to guard privateers in foreign sympathizing ports, as well as to care for every part of our own coast. They have taken forts that military men said could not be taken; and a brave admiral, for the first time in the world's history, lashed himself to the mast, there to remain as long as he had a particle of skill or strength to watch over his ship, while it engaged in the perilous contest of taking the strong forts of the rebels.

Then, again, I turn to the treasury department. Where should the money come from? Wise men predicted ruin, but our national credit has been maintained, and our currency is safer to-day than it ever was before. Not only so, but through our national bonds, if properly used, we shall have a permanent basis for our currency, and an investment so desirable for capitalists of other nations that, under the laws of trade, I believe the centre of exchange will speedily be transferred from England to the United States.

But the great act of the mighty chieftain, on which his fame shall rest long after his frame shall moulder away, is that of giving freedom to a race. We have all been taught to revere the sacred characters. Among them Moses stands preëminently high. He received the law from God, and his name is honored among the hosts of heaven. Was not his greatest act the delivering of three millions of his kindred out of bondage? Yet we may assert that Abraham Lincoln, by his proclamation, liberated more enslaved people than ever Moses set free, and those not of his kindred or his race. Such a power, or such an opportunity, God has seldom given to man. When other events shall have been forgotten; when this world shall have become a network of republics; when every throne shall be swept from the face of the earth; when literature shall enlighten all minds; when the claims of humanity shall be recognized everywhere—this act shall still be conspicuous on the pages of history. We are thankful that God gave to Abraham Lincoln the decision and wisdom and grace to issue that proclamation, which stands high above all other papers which have been penned by uninspired men.

Abraham Lincoln was a good man. He was known as an honest, temperate, forgiving man; a just man; a man of noble heart in every way. As to his religious experience, I cannot speak definitely, because I was not privileged to know much of his private sentiments. My acquaintance with him did not give me the opportunity to hear him speak on those topics. This I know, however, he read the Bible frequently; loved it for its great truths and its profound teachings; and he tried to be guided by its precepts. He believed in Christ the Saviour of sinners; and I think he was sincere in trying to bring his life into harmony with the principles of revealed religion. Certainly if there ever was a man who illustrated some of the principles of pure religion, that man was our departed President. Look over all his speeches, listen to his utterances. He never spoke unkindly of any man. Even the rebels received no word of anger from him, and his last day illustrated in a remarkable manner his forgiving disposition. A dispatch was received that afternoon that Thompson and Tucker were trying to make their escape through Maine, and it was proposed to arrest them. Mr. Lincoln, however, preferred rather to let them quietly escape. He was seeking to save the very men who had been plotting his destruction. This morning we read a proclamation offering $25,000 for the arrest of these men as aiders and abettors of his assassination; so that, in his expiring acts, he was saying: "Father, forgive them, they know not what they do."

As a ruler, I doubt if any President has ever shown such trust in God, or in public documents so frequently referred to divine aid. Often did he remark to friends and to delegations that his hope for our success rested in his conviction that God would bless our efforts, because we were trying to do right. To the address of a large religious body he replied: "Thanks be unto God, who, in our national trials, giveth us the churches." To a minister who said he hoped the Lord was on our side, he replied, that it gave him no concern whether the Lord was on our side or not, for, he added, "I know the Lord is always on the side of right;" and with deep feeling added: "But God is my witness, that it is my constant anxiety and prayer that both myself and this nation should be on the Lord's side."

In his domestic life he was exceedingly kind and affectionate. He was a devoted husband and father. During his presidential term he lost his second son, Willie. To an officer of the army, he said, not long since: "Do you ever find yourself talking with the dead?" and added: "Since Willie's death, I catch myself every day involuntarily talking with him, as if he were with me." On his widow, who is unable to be here, I need only invoke the blessing of Almighty God that she may be comforted and sustained. For his son, who has witnessed the exercises of this hour, all that I can desire is that the mantle of his father may fall upon him.

Let us pause a moment in the lesson of the hour before we part. This man, though he fell by an assassin, still fell under the permissive hand of God. He had some wise purpose in allowing him so to fall. What more could he have desired of life for himself? Were not his honors full? There was no office to which he could aspire. The popular heart clung around him as around no other man. The nations of the world had learned to honor our chief magistrate. If rumors of a desired alliance with England be true, Napoleon trembled when he heard of the fall of Richmond, and asked what nation would join him to protect him against our government under the guidance of such a man. His fame was full, his work was done, and he sealed his glory by becoming the nation's great martyr for liberty.

He appears to have had a strange presentiment early in political life, that some day he would be President. You see it indicated in 1839. Of the slave power he said: "Broken by it I too may be; bow to it I never will. The probability that we may fail in the struggle ought not to deter us from the support of a cause which I deem to be just. It shall not deter me. If ever I feel the soul within me elevate and expand to those dimensions not wholly unworthy of its Almighty architect, it is when I contemplate the cause of my country, deserted by all the world besides, and I standing up, boldly and alone, and hurling defiance at her victorious oppressors. Here, without contemplating consequences, before high Heaven and in the face of the world, I swear eternal fidelity to the just cause, as I deem it, of the land of my life, my liberty, and my love." And yet, recently, he said to more than one: "I never shall live out the four years of my term. When the rebellion is crushed my work is done." So it was. He lived to see the last battle fought, and dictate a dispatch from the home of Jefferson Davis; lived till the power of the rebellion was broken; and then, having done the work for which God had sent him, angels, I trust, were sent to shield him from one moment of pain or suffering, and to bear him from this world to the high and glorious realm where the patriot and the good shall live forever.

His career teaches young men that every position of eminence is open before the diligent and the worthy. To the active men of the country, his example is an incentive to trust in God and do right. To the ambitious there is this fearful lesson: of the four candidates for Presidential honors in 1860, two of them—Douglas and Lincoln—once competitors, but now sleeping patriots, rest from their labors; Bell, abandoned to perish in poverty and misery, as a traitor might perish; and Breckinridge is a frightened fugitive, with the brand of traitor on his brow.

Standing, as we do to-day, by his coffin and his sepulchre, let us resolve to carry forward the policy which he so nobly begun. Let us do right to all men. Let us vow, in the sight of Heaven, to eradicate every vestige of human slavery; to give every human being his true position before God and man; to crush every form of rebellion, and to stand by the flag which God has given us. How joyful that it floated over parts of every State before Mr. Lincoln's career was ended. How singular that, to the fact of the assassin's heels being caught in the folds of the flag, we are probably indebted for his capture. The flag and the traitor must ever be enemies.

Traitors will probably suffer by the change of rulers, for one of sterner mould, and who himself has deeply suffered from the rebellion, now wields the sword of justice. Our country, too, is stronger for the trial. A republic was declared by monarchists too weak to endure a civil war; yet we have crushed the most gigantic rebellion in history, and have grown in strength and population every year of the struggle. We have passed through the ordeal of a popular election while swords and bayonets were in the field, and have come out unharmed. And now, in our hour of excitement, with a large minority having preferred another man for President, when the bullet of the assassin has laid our President prostrate, has there been a mutiny? Has any rival proffered his claims? Out of an army of near a million, no officer or soldier uttered one note of dissent, and, in an hour or two after Mr. Lincoln's death, another leader, under constitutional forms, occupied his chair, and the government moved forward without one single jar. The world will learn that republics are the strongest governments on earth.

And now, my friends, in the words of the departed, "with malice towards none, free from all feelings of personal vengeance, yet believing that the sword must not be borne in vain," let us go forward even in painful duty.

Let every man who was a senator or representative in Congress, and who aided in beginning this rebellion, and thus led to the slaughter of our sons and daughters, be brought to speedy and to certain punishment. Let every officer educated at the public expense, and who, having been advanced to high position, perjured himself, and turned his sword against the vitals of his country, be doomed to a traitor's death. This, I believe, is the will of the American people. Men may attempt to compromise and to restore these traitors and murderers to society again. Vainly may they talk of the fancied honor or chivalry of these murderers of our sons—these starvers of our prisoners—these officers who mined their prisons and placed kegs of powder to destroy our captive officers. But the American people will rise in their majesty and sweep all such compromises and compromisers away, and will declare that there shall be no safety for rebel leaders. But to the deluded masses, we will extend the arms of forgiveness. We will take them to our hearts, and walk with them side by side, as we go forward to work out a glorious destiny.

The time will come when, in the beautiful words of him whose lips are now forever sealed, "The mystic cords of memory, stretching from every battle-field and patriot grave to every living heart and hearthstone all over this broad land, will yet swell the chorus of the Union, when again touched, as surely they will be, by the better angels of our nature."

Chieftain! farewell. The nation mourns thee. Mothers shall teach thy name to their lisping children. The youth of our land shall emulate thy virtues. Statesmen shall study thy record, and learn lessons of wisdom. Mute though thy lips be, yet they still speak. Hushed is thy voice, but its echoes of liberty are ringing through the world, and the sons of bondage listen with joy. Prisoned thou art in death, and yet thou art marching abroad, and chains and manacles are bursting at thy touch. Thou didst fall not for thyself. The assassin had no hate for thee. Our hearts were aimed at, our national life was sought. We crown thee as our martyr—and humanity enthrones thee as her triumphant son. Hero, Martyr, Friend, FAREWELL.

[The following beautiful hymn, accompanied by a band of music, was, among others, sung prior to the delivery of the preceding sermon.]

TRUST IN GOD.

Peace, troubled soul, thou need'st not fear;
Thy great Provider still is near;
Who fed thee last, will feed thee still:
Be calm, and sink into his will.

The Lord, who built the earth and sky,
In mercy stoops to hear thy cry;
His promise all may freely claim:
Ask and receive in Jesus' name.

Without reserve give Christ your heart;
Let him his righteousness impart;
Then all things else he'll freely give;
With him you all things shall receive.

Thus shall the soul be truly blest,
That seeks in God his only rest;
May I that happy person be,
In time and in eternity.

THE STAR-SPANGLED BANNER.

Oh, say, can you see, by the dawn's early light,
  What so proudly we hailed at the twilight's last gleaming?
Whose broad stripes and bright stars, through the perilous fight,
  O'er the ramparts we watched, were so gallantly streaming,
And the rockets' red glare, the bombs bursting in air,
  Gave proof through the night that our flag was still there:
    Oh, say, does that star-spangled banner yet wave
    O'er the land of the free and the home of the brave?

On that shore dimly seen through the mists of the deep,
  Where the foe's haughty host in dread silence reposes,
What is that which the breeze, o'er the towering steep,
  As it fitfully blows, now conceals, now discloses?
Now it catches the gleam of the morning's first beam,
In full glory reflected now shines in the stream.
    'Tis the star-spangled banner, oh long may it wave
    O'er the land of the free and the home of the brave.

And where are the foes who so vauntingly swore
  That the havoc of war and the battle's confusion
A home and a country should leave us no more?
  Their blood has washed out their foul footsteps' pollution.
No refuge could save the hireling and slave
  From the terror of flight, or the gloom of the grave;
    And the star-spangled banner in triumph doth wave
    O'er the land of the free and the home of the brave.

Oh thus be it ever, when freemen shall stand
  Between their loved homes and the war's desolation!
Blest with victory and peace, may the heaven-rescued land
  Praise the power that hath made and preserved us a nation!
Then conquer we must, when our cause it is just,
  And this be our motto—"In God is our trust!"
    And the star-spangled banner in triumph shall wave
    O'er the land of the free and the home of the brave.

OUR GOD IS MARCHING ON.

BATTLE HYMN OF THE REPUBLIC.

As sung by Chaplain C. C. McCabe, while a prisoner in Libby, after hearing old Ben (the colored paper-seller in Richmond) cry out; "*Great news by the telegraph! Great battle at Gettysburg! Union soldiers gain the day!*" Upon hearing such glorious news, Chaplain McCabe sung this soul-stirring hymn, all the prisoners joining him heartily in the chorus, making the old prison-walls ring with "GLORY, GLORY, HALLELUJAH!"

Mine eyes have seen the glory of the coming of the Lord;
He is trampling out the vintage where the grapes of wrath are stored;
He hath loosed the fateful lightning of His terrible quick sword:
    His truth is marching on.
Chorus—Glory, glory, hallelujah!

I have seen him in the watch-fires of a hundred circling camps;
They have builded Him an altar in the evening dews and damps;
I have read his righteous sentence by the dim and flaring lamps:
    His day is marching on.
Chorus—Glory, glory, hallelujah!

I have read a fiery gospel, writ in burnished rows of steel,
"As ye deal with my contemners, so with you my grace shall deal;
Let the Hero, born of woman, crush the serpent with his heel,
    Since God is marching on."
Chorus—Glory, glory, hallelujah!

He has sounded forth the trumpet that shall never call retreat;
He is sifting out the hearts of men before his judgment-seat;
Oh, be swift, my soul, to answer Him! be jubilant, my feet:
    Our God is marching on.
Chorus—Glory, glory, hallelujah!

In the beauty of the lilies Christ was borne across the sea
With a glory in his bosom that transfigures you and me;
As he died to make men holy, LET US DIE TO MAKE MEN FREE,
    While God is marching on.
Chorus—Glory, glory, hallelujah!

SERMON ON THE MOUNT.

(Matthew V., VI., VII.)

[While Hon. John M. Clayton, of Delaware, was Secretary of State under President Zachary Taylor, I rode with him in a stage coach from Dover, Del., to the steamboat at Smyrna Landing. It was before daylight. There were several in the stage: all were disposed to listen to the statesman, who was proverbial for conversational powers. Among other topics the subject of Religion was introduced, and in this matter Mr. Clayton was the leading spirit. He remarked: "My dear mother was a Methodist to the day of her death, and a bright Christian. I am a firm believer in the Christian religion. At Washington we frequently meet with skeptical persons, and with them I often have spirited controversies. I have read many works on the Evidences of Christianity, and heard sermons preached on the same subject; *but nothing that I have ever heard or read has convinced me so thoroughly of the truth and divinity of religion as the Lord's Sermon on the Mount and the Lord's Prayer.*"

However remotely Mr. Clayton lived from the Christian standard practically, he was theoretically a Christian through life, and in death he clung to the cross and professed saving faith in the Redeemer, and no doubt felt often in life and in death how great is the blessing of a pious mother, who first taught him to lisp "Our Father which art in heaven."

"O wondrous power! how little understood!
Entrusted to the mother's mind alone
To fashion genius, form the soul for good."]

And seeing the multitudes, he went up into a mountain: and when he was set, his disciples came unto him. And he opened his mouth, and taught them, saying,

Blessed *are* the poor in spirit: for theirs is the kingdom of heaven. Blessed *are* they that mourn: for they shall be comforted. Blessed *are* the meek: for they shall inherit the earth. Blessed *are* they which do hunger and thirst after righteousness: for they shall be filled. Blessed *are* the merciful: for they shall obtain mercy. Blessed *are* the pure in heart: for they shall see God. Blessed *are* the peacemakers: for they shall be called the children of God. Blessed *are* they which are persecuted for righteousness' sake: for theirs is the kingdom of heaven. Blessed are ye when *men* shall revile you, and persecute *you*, and shall say all manner of evil against you falsely, for my sake. Rejoice, and be exceeding glad: for great *is* your reward in heaven: for so persecuted they the prophets which were before you.

Ye are the salt of the earth: but if the salt have lost his savour, wherewith shall it be salted? it is thenceforth good for nothing, but to be cast out, and to be trodden under foot of men. Ye are the light of the world. A city that is set on an hill cannot be hid. Neither do men light a candle, and put it under a bushel, but on a candlestick: and it giveth light unto all that are in the house. Let your light so shine before men, that they may see your good works, and glorify your Father which is in heaven.

Think not I am come to destroy the law, or the prophets: I am not come to destroy, but to fulfil. For verily I say unto you, Till heaven and earth pass, one jot or one tittle shall in no wise pass from the law, till all be fulfilled. Whosoever therefore shall break one of these least commandments, and shall teach men so, he shall be called the least in the kingdom of heaven: but whosoever shall do, and teach *them*, the same shall be called great in the kingdom of heaven. For I say unto you, That except your righteousness shall exceed *the righteousness* of the scribes and Pharisees, ye shall in no case enter into the kingdom of heaven.

Ye have heard that it was said by them of old time, Thou shalt not kill; and whosoever shall kill, shall be in danger of the judgment: But I say unto you, that whosoever is angry with his brother without a cause, shall be in danger of the judgment: and whosoever shall say to his brother, Raca, shall be in danger of the council: but whosoever shall say, *Thou fool*, shall be in danger of hell-fire. Therefore, if thou bring thy gift to the altar, and there rememberest that thy brother hath aught against thee, leave there thy gift before the altar, and go thy way; first be reconciled to thy brother, and then come and offer thy gift. Agree with thine adversary quickly, while thou art in the way with him; lest at any time the adversary deliver thee to the judge, and the judge deliver thee to the officer, and thou be cast into prison. Verily I say unto thee, Thou shalt by no means come out thence, till thou hast paid the uttermost farthing.

Ye have heard that it was said by them of old time, Thou shalt not commit adultery: But I say unto you, That whosoever looketh on a woman to lust after her, hath committed adultery with her already in his heart. And if thy right eye offend thee, pluck it out, and cast *it* from thee: for it is profitable for thee that one of thy members should perish, and not *that* thy whole body should be cast into hell. And if thy right hand offend thee, cut it off, and cast *it* from thee: for it is profitable for thee that one of thy members should perish, and not *that* thy whole body should be cast into hell. It hath been said, Whosoever shall put away his wife, let him give her a writing of divorcement: But I say unto you, That whosoever shall put away his wife, saving for the cause of fornication, causeth her to commit adultery: and whosoever shall marry her that is divorced, committeth adultery.

Again ye have heard that it hath been said by them of old time, Thou shalt not forswear thyself, but shalt perform unto the Lord thine oaths: But I say unto you, Swear not at all: neither by heaven; for it is God's throne: Nor by the earth; for it is his footstool: neither by Jerusalem; for it is the city of the great King: Neither shalt thou swear by thy head, because thou canst not make one hair white or black. But let your communication be, Yea, yea; Nay, nay: for whatsoever is more than these cometh of evil.

Ye have heard that it hath been said, An eye for an eye, and a tooth for a tooth. But I say unto you, That ye resist not evil: but whosoever shall smite thee on thy right cheek, turn to him the other also. And if any man will sue thee at the law, and take away thy coat, let him have *thy* cloak also. And whosoever shall compel thee to go a mile, go with him twain. Give to him that asketh thee, and from him that would borrow of thee, turn not thou away.

Ye have heard that it hath been said, Thou shalt love thy neighbour, and hate thine enemy: But I say unto you, Love your enemies, bless them that curse you, do good to them that hate you, and pray for them which despitefully use you, and persecute you; that ye may be the children of your Father which is in heaven: for he maketh his sun to rise on the evil and on the good, and sendeth rain on the just and on the unjust. For if ye love them which love you, what reward have ye? do not even the publicans the same? And if ye salute your brethren only, what do ye more *than others?* do not even the publicans so? Be ye therefore perfect, even as your Father which is in heaven is perfect.

Take heed that ye do not your alms before men, to be seen of them: otherwise ye have no reward of your Father which is in heaven. Therefore, when thou doest *thine* alms, do not sound a trumpet before thee, as the hypocrites do, in the synagogues, and in the streets, that they may have glory of men. Verily I say unto you, They have their reward. But when thou doest alms, let not thy left hand know what thy right hand doeth; that thine alms may be in secret: and thy Father which seeth in secret, himself shall reward thee openly.

And when thou prayest, thou shalt not be as the hypocrites *are:* for they love to pray standing in the synagogues, and in the corners of the streets, that they may be seen of men. Verily I say unto you, They have their reward. But thou, when thou prayest, enter into thy closet, and when thou hast shut thy door, pray to thy Father which is in secret; and thy Father, which seeth in secret, shall reward thee openly. But when ye pray, use not vain repetitions, as the heathen *do:* for they think that they shall be heard for their much speaking. Be ye not therefore like unto them: for your Father knoweth what things ye have need of before ye ask him. After this manner therefore pray ye:

Our Father which art in heaven, hallowed be thy name. Thy kingdom come. Thy will be done in earth as it is in heaven. Give us this day our daily bread. And forgive us our debts, as we forgive our debtors. And lead us not into temptation, but deliver us from evil. For thine is the kingdom, and the power, and the glory, for ever. Amen.

For if ye forgive men their trespasses, your heavenly Father will also forgive you: but if ye forgive not men their trespasses, neither will your Father forgive your trespasses.

Moreover, when ye fast, be not as the hypocrites, of a sad countenance: for they disfigure their faces, that they may appear unto men to fast. Verily I say unto you, They have their reward. But thou, when thou fastest, anoint thine head, and wash thy face; that thou appear not unto men to fast, but unto thy Father which is in secret: and thy Father which seeth in secret shall reward thee openly.

Lay not up for yourselves treasures upon earth, where moth and rust doth corrupt, and where thieves break through and steal: but lay up for yourselves treasures in heaven, where neither moth nor rust doth corrupt, and where thieves do not break through nor steal. For where your treasure is, there will your heart be also. The light of the body is the eye: if therefore thine eye be single, thy whole body shall be full of light. But if thine eye be evil, thy whole body shall be full of darkness. If therefore the light that is in thee be darkness, how great *is* that darkness!

No man can serve two masters: for either he will hate the one, and love the other; or else he will hold to the one, and despise the other. Ye cannot serve God and mammon. Therefore I say unto you, Take no thought for your life, what ye shall eat, or what ye shall drink; nor yet for your body, what ye shall put on. Is not the life more than meat, and the body than raiment? Behold the fowls of the air: for they sow not, neither do they reap, nor gather into barns; yet your heavenly Father feedeth them. Are ye not much better than they? Which of you by taking thought can add one cubit unto his stature? And why take ye thought for raiment? Consider the lilies of the field, how they grow; they toil not, neither do they spin; and yet I say unto you, That even Solomon in all his glory was not arrayed like one of these. Wherefore, if God so clothe the grass of the field, which to-day is, and to-morrow is cast into the oven, *shall he* not much more *clothe* you, O ye of little faith? Therefore take no thought, saying, What shall we eat? or, What shall we drink? or, Wherewithal shall we be clothed? (For after all these things do the Gentiles seek): for your heavenly Father knoweth that ye have need of all these things. But seek ye first the kingdom of God, and his righteousness; and all these things shall be added unto you. Take therefore no thought for the morrow: for the morrow shall take thought for the things of itself. Sufficient unto the day *is* the evil thereof.

Judge not, that ye be not judged. For with what judgment ye judge, ye shall be judged: and with what measure ye mete, it shall be measured to you again. And why beholdest thou the mote that is in thy brother's eye, but considerest not the beam that is in thine own eye? Or how wilt thou say to thy brother, Let me pull out the mote out of thine eye; and behold, a beam *is* in thine own eye? Thou hypocrite, first cast out the beam out of thine own eye; and then shalt thou see clearly to cast out the mote out of thy brother's eye.

Give not that which is holy unto the dogs, neither cast ye your pearls before swine, lest they trample them under their feet, and turn again and rend you.

Ask, and it shall be given you; seek, and ye shall find; knock, and it shall be opened unto you: for every one that asketh, receiveth; and he that seeketh, findeth; and to him that knocketh, it shall be opened. Or what man is there of you, whom if his son ask bread, will he give him a stone? Or if he ask a fish, will he give him a serpent? If ye then, being evil, know how to give good gifts unto your children, how much more shall your Father which is in heaven give good things to them that ask him? Therefore all things whatsoever ye would that men should do to you, do ye even so to them: for this is the law and the prophets.

Enter ye in at the strait gate; for wide *is* the gate, and broad *is* the way, that leadeth to destruction, and many there be which go in thereat: because, strait *is* the gate, and narrow *is* the way, which leadeth unto life, and few there be that find it.

Beware of false prophets, which come to you in sheep's clothing, but inwardly they are ravening wolves. Ye shall know them by their fruits: Do men gather grapes of thorns, or figs of thistles? Even so every good tree bringeth forth good fruit; but a corrupt tree bringeth forth evil fruit. A good tree cannot bring forth evil fruit, neither *can* a corrupt tree bring forth good fruit. Every tree that bringeth not forth good fruit is hewn down, and cast into the fire. Wherefore, by their fruits ye shall know them.

Not every one that saith unto me, Lord, Lord, shall enter into the kingdom of heaven; but he that doeth the will of my Father which is in heaven. Many will say to me in that day, Lord, Lord, have we not prophesied in thy name? and in thy name have cast out devils? and in thy name done many wonderful works? And then will I profess unto them, I never knew you: depart from me, ye that work iniquity.

Therefore, whosoever heareth these sayings of mine, and doeth them, I will liken him unto a wise man, which built his house upon a rock: and the rain descended, and the floods came, and the winds blew, and beat upon that house; and it fell not: for it was founded upon a rock. And every one that heareth these sayings of mine, and doeth them not, shall be likened unto a foolish man, which built his house upon the sand: and the rain descended, and the floods came, and the winds blew, and beat upon that house; and it fell: and great was the fall of it.

And it came to pass when Jesus had ended these sayings, the people were astonished at his doctrine. For he taught them as *one* having authority, and not as the scribes.

"Praise God, from whom all blessings flow;
Praise Him, all creatures here below;
Praise Him above, ye heavenly host;
Praise Father, Son, and Holy Ghost."

www.ingramcontent.com/pod-product-compliance
Lightning Source LLC
Chambersburg PA
CBHW031349160426
43196CB00007B/782